TESTIMONIA

To read *Unplug Your Mind* is not to read
connect with the experience of Truth itself. Truth is expressed in these sacred pages and filters into the soul to re-wire, transmit and transmute wisdom into the heart. I recommend taking time to read slowly, breathe and settle into stillness after each passage as your awakening unfolds into the subtle realms. *Unplug Your Mind* enriched my experience of life as I gained insightful understanding from the messages of each Master. What a blessing to have this timely gift to guide our life's journey into wholeness.

Kia Scherr
President, One Life Alliance
www.onelifealliance.org

The Buddha, Jesus, Ezekiel, Abraham, Babaji... Open this book anywhere and you will find the living light of the Masters. Forget what you know or think you know. Take a deep breath and unplug from the matrix that holds so many people prisoner. Read the passages out loud. Let your soul drink in these vital messages. Feel the living vibrations in the words. And then use the energy and the wisdom to aid you in being your Real True Self.

Dan Brulé
www.breathmastery.com

Epic on a meta-galactic level!
I now understand the true meaning of "Christmas"; with gleeful anticipation, unwrapping presents from the Cosmic Mind; *Christ-in-mass*; one at a time! As I scrolled down the pages of *Unplug Your Mind* to reveal the first master, the message gradually unfolded. I likened this gradual revealing to the sense of taste of the finest chocolates. My soul experienced subtle energetic delicacies of infinite proportions!
This is not a book; it is an *initiation*!

After receiving this book in the morning, I opened the file and pulled down the bar at the side. The first word I saw was "Krishna." In that moment a massive wave of deep emotion engulfed my heart causing me to cease all activity and just sit in this Divine Energy as the air was forced out of my lungs. Eyes stretched wider than saucers, I returned to the beginning. As I read through the messages my feet were becoming uncomfortably hot; the carpet felt like black sand on a hot day – at one point I was up on my big toes! Body vibrating and melting, I felt like "Neo" from the Matrix movie after he comes up gasping from his first program download. I was integrating so much my neocortex felt like it had been completely rearranged – I felt like a machine! I had to laugh; one message said, "You are not a machine." It turned out the master was correct, by 6pm I was shattered! I lay back on the couch for a moment but immediately passed out till 12:45am with no wake, no dreamtime; silence. I *never* sleep during this time! I dared not read more and after feeding my baby Mia, got back to sleep at 2:45am.

I continued in the morning. Every single message was deeply profound and had a different feel. I was amazed at how much of the Divine Plan was revealed; some messages purely exhilarating. One of the messages spoke of alkalinizing the body; I found it curious that, through no action of my own, a reverse osmosis alkaline water filter had manifested in the house just a week prior.

Over the time I read the messages waves of light-headedness came through me as my heart center released blockages; I felt quite dizzy at times. For every message from the Council of AH, I felt the need to take a BIG full breath upon completion. They were all very intense.

At message 105 from the Great Father Tah-Tah, I experienced such an intense, overwhelming feeling of longing in my heart, I was deeply moved. Message 106 from the Great Mother Omah; the moment I began the message Mia called out. She had awaked for her next feed. It was 10:10pm. I was in such an emotional state of ecstasy when I lifted her out of the pram and held her up. I felt so much love for her I felt I was looking into Divine Mother's eyes. We laughed together for a while and fed before I completed the remaining messages.

I have been honored by many in my life. The opportunity to read through these sacred messages and give feedback is an honor for which I have no words...

In deepest gratitude and respect,

Jake Sole
Founder of Human Metamorphosis
www.humanmetamorphosis.com

I was honored to be asked to translate *Unplug Your Mind*. I felt privileged to support the offering of these messages from the masters and source that manifested through the love and dedicated focus of Ivonne Delaflor and Sylvia Dokter. The energetic transmission that flowed through these messages activated within me a felt sense of a deep connection to limitless love from which they flowed: Source and the Masters. It all made perfect sense, as each message was revealed and the translation just flowed in perfect balance and harmony.

The messages themselves are unique, powerful, and full of wisdom. They are a revelation, a doorway to perceive the preconceived reality in a new, vast, loving, limitless and ever expanding way.

This book is an open invitation from all these light evolved, guardian beings for us to unplug from all that it is not: from fear based beliefs, from the dark matrix and from programs and limitations that have obscured the embodiment of our true essence as co-creators of existence and divine beings.

I say yes to unplug. I say yes to what these beloved beings are sharing with us. I say yes to the awakening of humanity as presented in these messages. I say yes to these ultimate truths of existence.

My gratitude to my dear friends and soul companions on this ever amazing journey, Ivonne Delaflor and Sylvia Dokter for being a venue through which Humanity can benefit and rise with the messages from the ascended masters.

Claudia Molina Basteris
Author of *Tantra, the Art of Sacred Sexuality as a Gateway to Ascension*.

Unplug Your Mind is an astounding book of distilled messages and wake-up calls coming from the finer realms. Its abundance of incisive insights and transmissions is guaranteed to leave you energized and stunned for a while! A true delicacy to savor and assimilate one page at a time."

Karim Taleb, Ph.D

Following the advice of Sylvia Dokter, co author of *Unplug Your Mind*, I began to read this book sequentially, from the beginning. I thought I would read a few pages per day. However, in my flight from Cancun to the USA, I could not stop reading it and completed it by the time the plane landed. I felt as if I was transported to the higher dimension while reading. I felt a powerful energy transmission from each word in the book. This is a book I have been waiting for, to awaken humanity from a dreaming state which we are in for a long time. Of course, I will read it again and again, and I am sure that I will experience it in the deeper and different level. Thank you Ivonne and Sylvia for your contribution for humanity by bringing these most important messages to us in our time.

Toshie Yoneyama

I had the privilege of reading an advanced copy of *Unplug Your Mind*. If you are on a path of enlightenment or ascension then this book will be like water in a desert for you. The 108 messages contained within it will resonate deep inside you and ignite your power and drive to embody and fulfill your unique soul's mission. You've waited a long time for this, don't wait a moment longer. Read it now, and step up to do your part in the Great Awakening.

Steve Fulop
www.stairwaytonow.com

I have been reading many of Ivonne Delaflor Alexander's books this past year and all of them are an incredible contribution to humanity. When

I heard Ivonne was co writing a new book with Sylvia Dokter called *Unplug Your Mind*, I was anxiously awaiting for the opportunity to read it as I knew intuitively that this book was going to be big. After reading it I will say that this book was not only "big", it is on a whole other level!! Each message is an incredibly deep transmission of the great changes that await humanity! All my thoughts literally stopped as I was in complete awe after reading many of the messages. I truly believe that this book has challenged the way I think of my reality in many ways. I am currently on my third read through and each time I read it, the messages take on a deeper meaning. Thank you Ivonne and Sylvia for this wonderful contribution to humanity. One that I know I will be thoroughly enjoying for many years to come.

James Martinez

Reading the book *Unplug Your Mind* by Ivonne Alexander and Sylvia Dokter is an exceptional journey into all that is possible and available. The messages from each master are profound teachings that stand alone as well as create the experience of the integrated whole. The turning of each page leads onward and inward as I read with delight and understanding. Understanding that leads to confirmation, deeper awareness and embodiment of the multi-layered messages. The teachings show the way for all who choose to say Yes! Yes! Yes!

Mary Rocha.

As so many of the other classes, books and experiences I have had with the Higher School of Conscious Evolution, this book *Unplug Your Mind* takes understanding of my relationship with the sacredness of life to yet another higher level. Without having to understand every message, the totality of it leaves room for personal introspection. As well, *Unplug Your Mind* is a personal challenge to rise to the occasion of reaching for the truth of being.
With love and gratitude,

Patricia Brandon

UNPLUG YOUR MIND!

Messages from the Ascended Masters

Ivonne Delaflor Alexander
and Sylvia Dokter

Foreword by Toby Alexander
author of *The Great Master*

Unplug Your Mind!
Messages from the Ascended Masters

Copyright © 2013 Higher School for Conscious Evolution
Messages from the Ascended Masters © Ivonne Delaflor Alexander 2013
Commentaries made and copyrighted by Sylvia Dokter © 2013

All rights reserved. No part of this book may be used or reproduced by any means, graphic, electronic, or mechanical, including photocopying, recording, taping or by any information storage retrieval system without the written permission of the publisher except in the case of brief quotations embodied in critical articles and reviews.

iUniverse books may be ordered through booksellers or by contacting:

iUniverse
1663 Liberty Drive
Bloomington, IN 47403
www.iuniverse.com
1-800-Authors (1-800-288-4677)

The statements in this book have not been evaluated by the Food and Drug Administration. Products, services, suggestions, The Codes of AH©, *Unplug Your Mind! Messages From The Ascended Masters©* book, and any information provided here, are not intended to diagnose, treat, cure, or prevent any disease or mental illness. If you have a medical condition or an emotional imbalance, consult with your physician or therapist. All information provided here is for educational purposes only.

The messages here were received by Ivonne through the process of automatic writing.

Because of the dynamic nature of the Internet, any web addresses or links contained in this book may have changed since publication and may no longer be valid. The views expressed in this work are solely those of the author and do not necessarily reflect the views of the publisher, and the publisher hereby disclaims any responsibility for them.

Any people depicted in stock imagery provided by Thinkstock are models, and such images are being used for illustrative purposes only.

Certain stock imagery © Thinkstock.

ISBN: 978-1-4759-7432-4 (sc)
ISBN: 978-1-4759-7433-1 (e)

Library of Congress Control Number: 2013902414

Printed in the United States of America

iUniverse rev. date: 02/26/2013

Dedicated to all sentient beings and
the ascended universal family.

CONTENTS

Acknowledgments.. xvii

Foreword, by Toby Alexander, President of DNA Perfection xix

Why And How This Book Was Created, by Sylvia Dokter xxi

Introduction, by Ivonne Delaflor Alexander xxvii

Listening To The Masters, by Ivonne Delaflor Alexander......... xxxv

Message From Hermes, as received by Ivonne Delaflor Alexander .. xxxix

Part I – The Universal Awakening, as received by Ivonne Delaflor Alexander.................................. 1

Messages:
1. By Sri Mataji.. 3
2. By Sri Babaji Nagaraj...................................... 4
3. By Lord Kuthumi.. 5
4. The Cosmos, By Lord Matreya............................ 6
5. By Lord Matreya... 7
6. By Sri Babaji Nagaraj...................................... 8
7. By Lady Nada.. 9
8. By St Germaine.. 10
9. By Brother Issa.. 11
10. By The Council of AH................................... 12
11. By St Germaine... 13
12. By The Council of AH................................... 14
Commentary by Sylvia Dokter 15

Part II – The Death Of Politics, as received by Ivonne Delaflor Alexander.................................. 17

Messages:
13. By Lord Matreya... 19
14. By Master Kybalion 20

15. By Kwan Yin 21
16. By Sri Babaji Nagaraj 22
17. By Sri Babaji Nagaraj 23
18. By Lord Matreya 24
19. By Kwan Yin 25
20. By Sri Babaji Nagaraj 26
21. By Sri Babaji Nagaraj 27
22. By Babaji Nagaraj 28
Commentary by Sylvia Dokter 29

Part III – Reconnection With Earth, as received by Ivonne Delaflor Alexander 31

Messages:
23. By Kwan Yin 33
24. By Lady Nada 34
25. By The Council of AH 35
26. By The Council of AH 36
27. By Lord Matreya 37
28. By St Germaine 38
29. By Master Ebeelon 39
30. By Sri Mataji 40
31. By Hilarion 41
32. By Lord Kuthumi 42
33. By St Germaine 43
34. By Kwan Yin 44
35. By Sri Babaji Nagaraj 45
36. By Brother Issa 46
37. By The Council of AH 47
38. By Master Metatron 48
39. By Master Kybalion 49
40. By Master Hilarion 50
41. By Sri Babaji Nagaraj 51
42. By Sri Babaji Nagaraj 52
43. By Kwan Yin 53
Commentary by Sylvia Dokter 54

Part IV – Transition As A Higher Evolved Species, as received by Ivonne Delaflor Alexander 57

Messages:
44. By Lord Matreya... 59
45. By Grand Father Jaguar 60
46. By The Community at the Service of the Great Father of Sirius. . . 61
47. By Cuathli Aguila Exche 62
48. By Kwan Yin 63
49. By The Ahu, Rah Gestalt 64
50. By Brother Issa 65
51. By The White Brotherhood Gestalt................... 67
52. By Abraham... 68
53. By Lord Kuthumi.. 70
54. By Mary Magdalene..................................... 71
Commentary by Sylvia Dokter 73

Part V – Unplug Parental Programs, as received by Ivonne Delaflor Alexander 75

Messages:
55. By St Germaine.. 77
56. By Sri Babaji Nagaraj................................... 78
57. By Lord Kuthumi.. 79
58. By Kwan Yin 80
59. By Lord Matreya.. 81
60. By Lady Nada 83
61. By St Germaine.. 85
62. By Brother Isaiah 87
63. By Buddha 89
64. By Ezekiel 91
65. By Abraham... 93
66. By Brother Issa 95
Commentary by Sylvia Dokter 96

Part VI – Enlightenment, as received by Ivonne Delaflor Alexander 99

Messages:
67. By MA 101
68. The Star Gate Of The Seven Points By Brother Djwal 103
69. By J.K 105
70. The Divine Neutrality By Siddharta 106
71. Kingdom Of Celestial Wisdom By Serapis Bay 107
72. Freedom To Be By Lord Matreya 108
73. By Lady Nada 109
74. Remove Your Hidden Envy By Sanat Kumara 110
75. The Return Of The Goddess By Lady Nada 111
76. To Live Awake One Must Do What Is Right Consistently By St Germaine 112
77. Dropping The Ego By Kwan Yin 113
Commentary by Sylvia Dokter 114

Part VII – THe Secret Societies, as received by Ivonne Delaflor Alexander 117

Messages:
78. By Brother Paul.. 119
79. By Mary 120
80. By Father Hu-Nab, Kum................................. 121
81. By M.Krishna 123
Commentary by Sylvia Dokter 124

Part VIII – The Ascended Angels Speak, as received by Ivonne Delaflor Alexander...................... 125

Messages:
82. Prepare To Heal By Gabriel 127
83. Angelic Cosmic Evolution By Michael.................... 128
84. By Rafael 129
Commentary by Sylvia Dokter 130

Part IX – Wisdom From The Beyond, as received by Ivonne Delaflor Alexander 131

Messages:
85. By Kwan Yin 133
86. By Rah-Mah-El.. 134
87. By Ah-Mon-Rha... 135
88. By Isis 136
89. By The Nameless 137
Commentary by Sylvia Dokter 138

Part X – The Council Of AH, as received by Ivonne Delaflor Alexander 139

Messages:
90. By Equileh Ah Rah Meh Honorary Guardian Observant of The Laws of AH.. 141
91. By Sath, Kam AH First Officer of the Council of AH 142
92. By Gah-Ehl-Rah Master Emissary of Mind-physics of AH .. 143
93. By Ha-Ehl-Yeh AH Guardian of Universal Emissaries of Light Council of AH 144
94. By Eh-Nah-Yah-El Quantum Scholar Council of AH 145
95. By Kah-Mah-Ehl Wisdom Elder Council of AH 146
96. By Ah-Mhan-Tat Great Father Founder Council of AH 147
97. By Babaji Nagaraj Ascended Master Representative Guest at the Council of AH 148
98. By Lha-Tzah-Eh Honorary Member, Council of AH........ 149
99. By Hay Merth Hau Hu Honorary Guardian of the Law of Cause and Effect, Member of the Council of AH 150
100. By Mataji Guest Honorary Earth mechanics Consultant for the Council of AH 151
101. By Yeshua Ha Yuh Guardian Omni Love Field Frequencies Counselor for The Council of AH 152
Commentary by Sylvia Dokter 153

Part XI – Scientists Of Universal Creation, as received by Ivonne Delaflor Alexander 155

Messages:
102. By Hunab Kah Hul Quantum Chief Soul Creator Medical Universal Scientist Guest Honor for the Council of AH 157
103. By Hel-Tha-Hu Universal Architect Engineer, Member of the Council of AH 159
104. By G-HAY-El-HI Physics Tao Guardian, Council of AH.... 160
Commentary by Sylvia Dokter 162

Part XII – Final Instructions For The Sons & Daughters Of Earth, as received by Ivonne Delaflor Alexander 163

Messages:
105. By The Father Tah-Tah, Great Founder Father of AH 165
106. By The Mother OMAH Great ONE Mother of AH 166
107. By Tah-Tah-Yeh Great Grandfather Founder of Gaia........ 168
108. By Eah-Rtha Gestalt Founder Mothers & Fathers of Earth .. 169
Commentary by Sylvia Dokter 170

Visualization To Be Used With The Matrix Unplug Stage I Code of AH© By Sylvia Dokter................................ 171

Epilogue, by Ivonne Delaflor Alexander..................... 173

Ascended Masters References 174

About The Authors
  Ivonne Delaflor Alexander 185
  Sylvia Dokter... 187

Other Books By the Authors................................. 189

Suggested Reading To Further Your Connection With Higher Worlds 194

Notes.. 197

ACKNOWLEDGMENTS

We thank the ascended masters, gestalt consciousness, and councils in all realms for their support, love, and revelation of the higher truths that can support mankind during this important stage of the shift of planetary and collective consciousness.

We give special thanks to the following persons, whose support contributed to the co-creation of this book:

Linda Heller (Swami Bharatananda), who, with relentless patience, was in charge of the grammatical editing.
Claudia Molina (Swami Ananda), who translated the book in Spanish with adamant focus and clarity.
Toby Alexander (Swami Shivananda Brahmananda), world wide DNA Activation authority who gifted us with a powerful foreword and presence during the co-creation of this book.

We thank Planet Earth for hosting us in this most auspicious time for humanity.

And we thank you, reader of this book, for your willingness to evolve and contribute to the unplugging of illusions and for embracing the embodiment of pure pristine essence during the cycle of ascension and human evolution in the now.

From our hearts to yours;
Thank You

Ivonne Delaflor Alexander
&
Sylvia Dokter

FOREWORD

Imagine if every night you could connect to the highest ascended masters and receive messages that not only detail the process of ascension and what will occur in 2012 and beyond, but also expose the secrets of the hidden societies, governmental organizations, and those of the power elite.

Imagine if your mission is to receive these messages and distribute them to humanity for a massive global awakening at this very important time in Earth's history and that these same ascended beings depend on you for doing this.

For the past three months, I have been present in my wife's office from around 11:00pm until at least 1:00am watching her receive these messages and then watching her type them. For me it was incredible to watch and an amazing gift, not only of the transmission of energy but also the knowledge and wisdom that the messages contain. Imagine receiving guidance from the likes of Jesus, Babaji Nagaraj, Lord Maitreya, Hermes, Mary Magdalene, and many more ascended gestalts of consciousness on exactly what is and has been happening in our history and what to watch for in the coming months and years.

After she would type the messages she received and who it was from, she would then say to me: "Do you want to hear it"? And I would always say "Of course!". What am I going to say? "No, please do not share with me what the ascended masters and mahavatars Jesus or Babaji said?"

It seemed like every message built on the previous one and they got more and more intense and exciting as they went.

Some of the messages were mind-stoppers: you read them and you just do not have any thoughts or words to say. That shows how powerful they are.

Just reading the messages is like receiving a shaktipat from a great master and as you go through the book, you will become aware of your frequency rising. Plus there are many messages that will completely annihilate your current belief systems about reality, religion, Earth history, politics, and who you truly are.

I can honestly say that out of all of the so-called spiritual texts out there, these messages are the most profound and the only ones that have not been tampered with or distorted, as Ivonne just typed the messages as they were given and served as a humble scribe. Yet in reality, it takes a special ability to be able to be entrained to this frequency and to handle the energy of the messages as well as connect to these beings, and Ivonne has this amazing ability to listen to the Intelligent Space.

I pay tribute to her commitment and consistency to receive these messages as she is an extremely busy mother with three children and late at night is the only time that she has for herself. The messages speak for themselves so there is really nothing else to be said. When this book gets out there, worldwide, many massive shifts in consciousness will take place.

These are the messages any committed spiritual seeker requires for the upcoming Golden Age of Enlightenment that we have been waiting eons for. I trust that you will have a phenomenal experience reading this book and that you will apply the messages in your own life for the highest good of yourself, your family, and the collective consciousness.

Omni-love,
Toby Alexander

President DNA Perfection
www.dnaperfection.com

WHY & HOW THIS BOOK WAS CREATED

I'm trying to free your mind, Neo. But I can only show you the door. You're the one that has to walk through it.
~ *Morpheus in the 1999 movie, The Matrix*

In August 2012, during the period where planetary and human changes were taking place, I felt honored to receive a special request from Sri Babaji Nagaraj,[1] an ascended master.[2]

I have had the privilege to receive direct guidance and/or requests from Babaji through telepathic communication before and most of the time I received them during dreamtime or by projected thought forms on my computer screen. In this particular message Babaji asked me to create a book together with Ivonne Delaflor Alexander, who is my dear friend

---

[1] Babaji is recognized in the spiritual world as the ageless Sidda (adept), omniscient, omnipotent and omnipresent who was introduced to Westerners in the book, *Autobiography of a Yogi*, written by Pramahansa Yogananda. The meaning in English for Babaji is "Venerable Father." It is said by those who have met Babaji, that he is the Param Sidda (Supreme Perfected Being) who has achieved a state free from death limitations. He can travel through time and space as he wishes with or without a physical body. Babaji is immortal. It is said that he never lives in the same place for more than seven days. He travels from place to place in the northern Himalayan Mountains with his select group of disciples. He easily can speak in any language. His immortal body does not require food; therefore he seldom eats. His mission is love. And it is said that when his name is pronounced with love, humbleness and reverence an immediate blessing is received. Om Babaji Namaha. www.maitriorder.com

[2] Ascended Masters are spiritual beings who once lived on earth and gained mastery over human limitations. They come from all different cultures and religions and are united in a gestalt called "The Great White Brotherhood." The term "white" refers to the white light and has nothing to do with race. They are the guides and teachers of mankind to support those desiring to master spiritual evolution.

and also my mentor and partner in several businesses. He added that this book was to be shared with humanity! I instantly said YES to this opportunity to serve the collective and called Ivonne. Considering this period, called Ascension, where the world is immersed with information, speculations and so called prophecy theories of what would happen in December 2012 and beyond, I understood the importance of supporting humanity by revealing TRUTH!

Ascension is not about the end of the world. No, ascension is about a collective conscious uplifting and spiritual evolving, up to the 15 dimensional time matrix and beyond. This is a natural cycle, also called the *Euiago cycle*, which takes place every 26500 years for humans, other species and planets. Earth and humanity are undergoing this conscious uplifting process now. This process takes place by accreting light into our energetic field, raising frequencies and activating the fire letters in our DNA template to ascend and attain the next corresponding dimension. In other words, the transformation of our world into a cooperative, compassionate, peaceful, harmonic, joyful environment where higher ethical values exist and the physical body is healthy and vital. This special request reminded me of the conversation I had with Babaji in the summer of 2009 in which he asked me to gather fifty-four messages and to create a book. The message was short and it was not clear for me at that time how the messages would come or from whom. Moreover I did not realize that this request would really manifest three years later.

Ivonne would receive the messages and my task was to add a commentary after each part about my own experience of walking through this sacred space. This three month period of gathering the messages was an uplifting experience for me. The messages directed me to contemplate, meditate and do deeper research. I gained more insights and clarity than before. Seeing reality with other eyes and perceptions; I experienced an increase of external awareness in my direct environment, in nature in dreams or through telepathic transmissions from the Intelligent Space. What resulted was an immense feeling of gratitude and joy and a stronger visualization of "happy faces" what the future represents for me.

I realized what a gift these messages, or transmissions, are for all of humanity.

Ivonne received the messages through telepathic transmission. I have been in her presence for some; she enters in a silent state and totally present, takes a deep breath, and suddenly starts writing, with one hand typing very fast without watching the screen. This was the first time I witnessed someone expressing automatic writing and it was an amazing experience. At the same time I heard like a "pfffeee" in my right ear, and goose bumps appeared all over the body as if I traveled into a different space with Ivonne.

There was an incredible synchronicity that took place upon the receipt of each message: when Ivonne received them I was at home working on the messages, doing research or meditating, or suddenly hearing sounds in my inner ear, doing a cleansing ritual in the ocean or somehow reading about ascension related to the messages we received…. As if a certain force field was created: A truly humbling and beautiful experience to realize this interconnectedness with multidimensional beings. I also learned that Toby[3], Ivonne's husband was present for most of the messages that Ivonne received late at night.

Upon reading the first message I realized that Ascension is about more than the ascension of the earth and humanity. This first shift is the beginning of an enormous universal uplifting. During the weeks that followed, my gratitude, awareness, and excitement kept increasing. The best way for me to integrate the transmissions that these messages are was to remain in longer periods of silence and not let myself be distracted by watching media inserted programs whose purpose is to instill fear and doubts.

Both Ivonne and I observed how our perceptions of our environment shifted. These were moments of great fun and it was with a sense of complicity we shared in a common joy-field. Upon receiving message fifty-four it became clear for us that the book was not finished and

---

[3] Toby Alexander. President of DNA Perfection and co-founder of the Higher School for Conscious Evolution. www.dnaperfection.com

more messages were to follow. About half way toward the completion of the book as my body entered its own awakening process, it began to manifest a divine fever and a cleansing through the nose and throat. To support the integration of the transmissions given by these messages, I highly recommend that you pause and drink a lot of water after reading message fifty-four.

These messages have clear recommendations and suggestions for how to unplug from this 15 dimensional time matrix system, where the mindset of humanity has been controlled for thousands of years through cultural and religious indoctrination. As a consequence humanity only uses 5 pct of its capabilities and lives by blindly following rules of indoctrination and limiting beliefs of what is possible instead of following one's soul purpose and personal freedom of choice.

To support the integration of these transmissions, Ivonne created a 12 stage Codes of AH© program. And she offered one of the codes as a gift to the readers of this book. You will find more information later in this book. Considering my experiences of applying these codes as a Codeologist, I can state that these messages combined with the use of the Codes of AH become a true threshold of ultimate support for the human family in this important stage of change.

I am grateful for this opportunity and I pay tribute to all Masters gifting us with these powerful messages: All those beautiful souls supporting, protecting, guiding with dedication and commitment to bring humanity and the Earth toward brilliancy. Specifically I would like to thank Babaji for his ever loving guidance and presence and for the honor and privilege I realized this "request" is to co-create a divine tool to support the human family. I am also aware that this gift was an opportunity to go deeper within myself. I was required to stretch my awareness and I felt how self-healing patterns increased. I thank my dear friend Ivonne for her energy and presence to walk this journey together. The moments of laughter, contemplations, amazement, and joy we shared by walking through renewed perceptions of reality and at the same time receiving her teachings are priceless.
Thank you!

These messages are meant for those who are ready to listen and most of all, who are ready to ACT upon them. Each of you will interpret the messages through the filter of your own level of awareness and willingness to unplug yourself from the matrix.

May this book support and inspire you to step up and find your own truth within as it did for me. Yet as always, the choice is yours.

In deep gratitude for these gifts,

Sylvia Dokter

INTRODUCTION

One big Yes, to life; is the end of all no's. ~ Eckhart Tolle

To be able to serve humanity is one of the most thrilling experiences in my life. I was honored, when my dear friend, business partner and Certified Master Trainer of the Transcendental Rebirthing System,[1] Sylvia Dokter shared with me a request she had received from an Ascended Master, Babaji Nagaraj for us to write a book together.

I was in the midst of publishing two new books, one on leadership, and another one about Father Energy, when this request came in. I had no idea how and what they were asking and how it would be delivered, I just said YES, that's all I did.

In the request Sylvia was told that we were to receive fifty-four messages that we were to share with our human family. I was going to receive the messages, and Sylvia would write a commentary, and an explanation of what the message created in her experience and what she sees in them.

Little did I know that this process was to begin immediately. Within 24 hours I began to receive messages late at night. These messages came through a process of automatic writing[4]. Messages that took me LITERALLY not only out of my comfort zone[5], but out of a concept I had of the world. After writing them, when I shared them with Sylvia,

---

[4] Automatic writing or psychography is the process, or product, of writing material that does not come from the conscious thoughts of the writer. The writer's hand forms the message, and the person is unaware of what will be written. It is sometimes done in a trance state. www.crystalinks.com

[5] A place or situation where one supposedly feels safe or at ease and without stress.

we discovered they were in perfect synchronicity[6] with whatever Sylvia was doing at the same time in her work, or at home.

One by on my beliefs[7] shattered, and oh what a joy! The stories, the memories, the emotions linked to the past, the history of humanity in religion, tragedies, war...all began to vanish.

Every night and sometimes during the day I would feel a pull, a call, and would immediately go to the computer and receive and type. No editing, no wondering if what was being received sounded pretty, made sense or not. My job was clear: to receive and type the messages... and that's exactly what I did.

After receiving the messages, sometimes one to four messages per night, I would re-read the messages to my husband and we both entered in a state of altered consciousness. All the words you could hear from both of us were: "Wow, oh...Huh?" ...and the rest was silence.

During the days the messages were received, everyday reality seemed to fade away. At least the "reality" I thought I was living, and a new reality emerged. A reality of presence and goodness, where my emotions were more engaged in the here and now. I let go of vesting my emotions in thoughts of suffering, desiring to end the war, and all that stuff that seems to me now to be a program for humanity to remain asleep.

I remember once in a workshop in Cancun many years ago, a teacher from the heart and dear friend, Alan Cohen, shared that Mother Theresa was being interviewed, and the journalist asked her: "So Mother Theresa, tell us your point of view, regarding war, are you against it?" Puzzled she looked back at the journalist, kept a moment of silence and then answered. "My dear friend, I am not against war, I am just in favor of Peace". This story now makes even more sense to me than before. The messages seem to unplug me from a collective tape that plays the repeat

---

[6] The simultaneous occurrence of events that appear significantly related but have no discernible causal connection.

[7] An acceptance that a statement is true or that something exists. Something one accepts as true or real; a firmly held opinión or conviction.

button again and again; a cycle of fear, suffering, poverty, oppression, victimization and so on.

Each message carried its own transmission, which deepened the unplugging process even more. Some of the messages were given by Ascended Masters, and some were given with names that we've never heard of before like Kybalion. Later on, Sylvia found out there was already a book written with that name. She was in charge of the research, me of receiving the messages and transmitting them in the written form. Yet we both experienced the unplugging simultaneously. Messages were validated during the whole day.

One time we were wondering, what would the name for the book be? We knew questions have power, so we allowed the question to sit. And then, there it was the answer! The next day Sylvia chose to post a picture in Facebook that said, "What the heck, unplug and have fun!" The same day, I received at 4 a.m. the name Unplugging after meditation. It was clear, the name of the book was being given; *Unplug Your Mind!*

And I am sure you will.
After completing the fifty-four messages as requested, messages kept coming, a total of 108 were finally received.

These messages have the power to break belief patterns. They also give multi-dimensional prophecies, which require a bigger and broader mind expansion to even grasp their essence. Though, whether you believe or not, whether you relate to a name or not, it won't really matter, as the transmission is beyond the words.

Part I: The Universal Awakening

This is a preparatory ground for the next messages. It announces the collective awakening not only of humans but also of the universal spirit. It prepares the field for the mind to let go of the old patterns created by a matrix[8] that has been placed in the human psyche. A matrix that has controlled the Earth and it peoples for thousands of years. Now is time for its completion.

---

[8] A mathematical environment or material in which something develops.

Part II: The Death of Politics

The title says it all: humanity will be required to raise its collective consciousness, unplug from the tyranny of fabricated genes, and awaken in to a leadership of spirit. The masters here guide us well. The masters teach us to look within in to our own collective, individual and family politics. They teach us the steps to take in order to liberate our souls and start walking the path of ascension in spirit.

Part III: The Reconnection with Earth

It is exactly that, an unveiling of the disconnection from what takes us away from a life of values and nature. It is a guide to the rebirth and reconnection with Mother Earth, here and now.

Part IV: Transitions as Higher Evolved Species

The messages here were, at least for us, the strongest messages. We received communications both from beings we were "used to" receiving spiritual data from and messages of beings that seemed to be Mayan Teachers and special councils.

Part V: Unplug Parental Programs

Amazing timely messages, for the most important portal in Humanity, which is the one of parenting. Guiding us to what matters most for the sake of children and the future civilizations, supporting us to remove, uplift and become evolved in mind, body and spirit and a pure embodiment of light and guidance for our future generations in the now.

Part VI: Enlightenment

An accurate guide on this most sought after topic and state of being for evolved human beings. Here the ideas and identifications with this state as a concept slowly vanish as the truth, which can't be spoken is transmitted beyond the messages.

Part VII: Messages for The Secret Societies

This section focuses upon communications directed to the societies that hold power either through secrecy, the control of spiritual beliefs or manipulation of others. Societies that utilize fear, or other forms of manipulation with the purpose of earthly and or mental domination over humanity. In a universe that is ascending and whose birth is based on truth, nothing can remain hidden from the open heart and awakened mind, and these messages bring light to this aspect of humanity.

Part VIII: The Ascended Angels Speak

Until this book I have never received communications from the archangels in a direct way. Usually it was through Doreen Virtue[9] whom I had the privilege to host in Cancun once for an Archangels workshop, or through different dreams, and visions. These messages tell us the process they are in, reminding us that everything evolves, the earth, the planets, all beings are in the process of evolution and ascension, and they give us their perspective on what is happening right now and how can we apply their experience in our own transcendental evolution.

Part IX: Wisdom from Beyond

These messages bypass " the concept of outside the box". They carry a transmission that is beyond the box. These messages re-calibrate our minds to a channel of pure receiving. A channel where the heart opens to new dimensions and the eternal truth that can't be spoken is received within the wholeness of our being.

---

[9] Author of *Goddesses & Angels*. In this book Doreen Virtue wrote a chapter about Ivonne Delaflor when Ivonne hosted her in Cancun, Mexico for an Archangels workshop.

Part X: The Council of AH

These messages are given from Higher Beings that work in Harmony from what is called the AH Universe[10]. Their benevolence, guidance and wisdom, invite all humans to transcend our limited concept of who we are. They invite us, as a species and as beings of infinite intelligence, to walk through the portal of ascension and become citizens of the Harmonic Universe.

Part XI: Scientists for Universal Creation

Here we see how mathematics plays a role in creation, how quantum physics is not only used on earth but through all realms and by all sentient beings.

Part XII: Final Instructions for the Sons & Daughters of Earth

Here, the final instructions, which in truth leave us with a taste for more. We can feel the embrace, the common sense aspect of the messages, we feel finally back Home.

These messages felt like an initiation that shifted our belief paradigms and activated our awakening process even more. All the messages have in common their focus in the awakening and support of humanity for the betterment of collective universal awakening.

All the messages seem to have the foundation of peace and a call for us to drop all fear, to trust, to love and unplug.

Love is seen here not only as a human emotion, but also as a higher counteracting program that will make the program of fear obsolete.

From the 1st message to the 108th, we were literally in another space, a space that we used to call another dimension, which seems now to be reality.

---

[10] Absolute Harmonic Universe. A universe which is beyond the 15 dimensional time matrix.

At the completion of message fifty-four, my body experienced a powerful fever and flu like symptoms, and I felt like a detox process was in place. I had not felt like this, except when I had done a heavy detox program. I remained eating raw foods, which seemed to help the process and the release of whatever was coming out from my preconceptions and matrix structured world. The food, daily meditating and consistent care of my body; mind and spirit seemed to support the integration and replenishment process; a huge release, a restoration, and an unplugging of a major order. The rest of the messages were received after a period of rest, the energy seemed stronger yet my body felt much at ease, my mind by now more open than ever before, like my heart…it is like the first fifty-four were preparing us for what was to come.

We don't come to share the messages to create a new prophetic text, or as a follow up to the Matrix movies, we come to share our "YES" to an assignment that seemed to have completed itself. We just offer our service as requested…the rest is up to you and existence itself.

We invite you to read the messages and allow their transmission to guide you to unplug from whatever is hindering your growth, to let go of old belief systems that no longer serve you as a god creator. To release old fears and self-limiting thought patterns, which do not allow you to unleash your soul potential for enlightenment and greatness.

We invite you to open your mind and heart and pause the judgment habit, take what serves you and disregard what doesn't.

I didn't add any further comments to the messages received, nor were they needed. What else could I say beyond what these beings of light or gestalts of consciousness had offered?

My silence is my sharing, and the messages do the talking, and hopefully they will create the necessary fuel to propel the inner star gate[11] of

---

[11] A star gate is essentially an enormous superconductor, capable of harnessing power from a wide variety of energy sources, especially electricity, capable of sending people and objects hundreds of thousands of light years via an interstellar conduit. www.urbandictionary.com

consciousness to be activated and ascend the human spirit towards more presence, more freedom, more love as Universal Beings in the Now.

May your unplugging be the ultimate celebration and tribute to the human spirit.

Human Family:

IT IS TIME!

In service to love,

Ivonne Delaflor Alexander
Author of *The Book of Origins*

LISTENING TO THE MASTERS

Everyone on Earth has formed special relationships, and although this is not so in heaven, the Holy Spirit knows how to bring a touch of Heaven to them here.
~ A Course In Miracles

Since early age, around 4 to be precise, I used to have what many have called outer body experiences and visitations, from beings, or "angels" as I used to call them. When I shared these events with my family their response "it is just your imagination" was no surprise.

As a small child, I learned to remain silent, to keep secret the everyday manifestations of these happenings that were considered by others, especially my family, to be "impossible" and examples of a "vivid imagination."

As the years went by the visitations and out of body experiences continued. When I entered my teens I listened less. Although a part of me felt the invitation of an inner calling a search, I bought into and became totally "plugged" into the glamour of the external signs of success, popularity and achievement: clothes, social status, popularity, and grades. On November 11, 1989, I had what many call a Near Death Experience. A friend and I had a major car "accident" (Now I call it a life incident) and my right arm was severed from my body. It was literally reattached to my body by an amazing doctor, Fortunate Reyes. My left leg's femur was totally fractured and needless to say, my life changed abruptly.

Weeks before this incident took place, as I was driving to school, I kept hearing a loud male voice saying: *Slow down*. Sometimes the voice was accompanied by the feeling of a strong earthquake. This feeling was strong enough for me to stop driving the car and ask my friends if they felt the earthquake, to which they responded: there was none!

I also had temporal moments where I could see nothing; blackness, that was more than the darkness that I was experiencing with my external eyes. A metaphor perhaps of what was coming and my ordinary mind couldn't see?

At the moment of the incident, I saw the car bending, folding in upon itself like a waded up paper. I saw my arm being detached from my body as the right window cut through it, I saw my femur coming out through the skin of my left leg, and besides these very physical experiences, what I remember the most was a golden brilliant light that was present at all times, infusing every moment.

This light was an all-intelligent field.

As the car stopped, and the impact came to completion…immediately; call it adrenaline, call it mind skills, or call it the intelligent field…I began to take action while imprisoned within a car that most definitely didn't look like a car anymore. My friend, who was driving my car that day, had lots of bruises and some shattered glass on her face, yet she was able to walk away from the crash and get support. However she began to panic and I had to take action and make decisions.

That same moment, a man was walking by and I was able to give to him precise instructions on whom to call, and what to do.

My mind knew all the information, the numbers of every single place and persons he needed to call, what hospital to tell the ambulance to take us to, as well as the phone numbers of my friend and her family. There was at all times a feeling of clarity, of certainty.

I was taken to the nearest hospital, called back then *The Angels*.

On call there was a specialist for arms and bone fractures.

Coincidence? I don't think so.

During this whole process, I could feel the presence of this field. This field has been here since that moment in very active communication with me.

A perfect setting created as an opportunity for me to change my life, and listen to the voice of source as God, serve it, allow it and share it.

Years passed, and my spiritual awakening grew stronger, my desire to serve was like an addiction, and events unfolded in my life as learning experiences. I traveled to India, where I was privileged to meet the immortal master; called Babaji that Yogananda speaks of in his book *Autobiography of a Yogi*. He spoke directly to me, as many other teachers have done, and materialized in front of my ordinary eyes.

After this India experience[12], I have received messages from the masters. Books like *Invitation to Love; 108 Messages for the Enlightened Ones. Sacred Messages for the Parents of the World*, co-authored with Swami Amarananda, The *Book of Origins* and now this book contain the information encoded in these messages. Messages have come from beings like St. Germaine, Mother Mary, and Babaji as well as beings I've never heard of before.

All these beings represent a gestalt of consciousness of service and love.

All are masters with one common goal: be of service and support humanity to evolve in to its own magnificence. I can tap at will in to the space now where they will speak, and sometimes they awaken me at 4 a.m. to dictate what they desire to share. Sharings and teachings that may support others let go of suffering, to find and activate their mission in order to live a life of passion, purpose, and happiness, which supports the whole.

I now do private readings where people can directly receive messages from the masters themselves and healings. In these readings, I serve as the translator or conduit for the sharing of these messages.

---

12 You can read more about Ivonne's India experience in her book: *India; The journey of a Lifetime*. Available at Amazon.com and all online retailers. In this book she shares where she met Mahavatar Babaji and her whole mystical journey along the way.

I also teach other people how to connect directly with these higher beings, or ascended masters, as I support them to recognize and learn how to listen to the Intelligent Space. A space that many call the Field, or Mind of God, and that was introduced to me by Babaji Nagaraj while writing the book *Sacred Messages for the Parents of the World*. (In this book I describe these experiences with detail).

I truly believe that what I do, can be done by everyone. Everyone can communicate with this sacred space. This communication requires willingness, a clear purpose and an agenda to be of service while holding the space of purity, poise, integrity, and grace.

Yes, the messages received in this book are not a mere coincidence, they are given to a receiver, that has said yes to serve, and has the willingness to listen and pass along whatever is in the highest good for mankind… for our human family.

Now let us begin….

MESSAGE FROM HERMES

October 27th, 2012 at 5:44 PM

*The Eight Universal Laws here are presented to thee,
in diverse instructions and expansive awakening calls.
Spoken in the different languages preferred by a mind that projects the
holographic universe[13], so the chosen ones can understand it.
Oh Seeker, Oh Lover of Truth, Oh Divine Alchemist
no coincidence that to the arms of the Divine thou have come.
What seem words are but whispers in thy soul that in its longing
has reached its destiny.
Dwell upon the light beyond the message.
Merge as the one and only recipient of these instructions.
Offer thy heart to the infinite presence of the space that contains the all,
the mind of the divine.
Oh Vessel of Illumination,
Masters, Teachers, Mothers, Fathers, Leaders, Rulers, Monks and Scholars
The gathering has begun.
The 144000 have been summoned.
The powers of the mental universe offer to the void with humility
an initiation door thou are about to enter.
Come barefoot,
Come thoughtless,
Come shapeless,*

---

[13] Universe formed by holograms. A hologram is a virtual image formed by light waves diverging from an apparant focus of source. *The Holographic Universe*, by Michael Talbot.

*To thee I offer the diversity of my 10,000 names.
Let thy spirit take action as thy mind surrenders.
Twelve gates thou shall walk
And then initiate others by thy mere loving presence.
Sharing this wisdom with those ready,
through the breath of life,
and the fire that has united the universal spirit.
Thou have come Home.*

Hermes

PART I
THE UNIVERSAL AWAKENING

Message 1
By Sri Mataji

August 28, 2012 - 11:09 AM

The Light of the Universe is to shine tenfold with the new luminaries being born from the ascension cycle of Earth.

The compassionate ones welcome thee all.
Oh ascended beings, the family of humans,
we welcome thee with eagerness and anticipation
as we collaborate with thee all in this co-creation of the New Earth,
and the next stage of ascension, which is universal.

We are but to take the first step by expressing gratitude,
as our councils merge as one.
Thy body adjusts to the change, and thy mind opens to
the infinite possibilities of THE ONE.

Message 2
By Sri Babaji Nagaraj

August 29, 2012 - 11:56 AM

*Humanity must start working together,
now that the shift has taken place,
in replenishing the green fields which are in reality
the heart chakra of Mother Nature.*

Children must return to the sacred abode of farming.

*The transition to universal status, is taking place effortlessly,
the new beings arriving, are to not distract the REAL beings
that protect Earth.*

*Many changes will take place: things veiled, now un-veiled
beings that change shapes, stepping forward.*

*Ah, I say to thee, distract not from the path of love.
Higher frequency has never existed of before.*

Message 3
By Lord Kuthumi

August 29, 2012 - 8:57 PM

As the grids on Earth align with the Pleiades[14], the pyramids and the ten stellar cycles that are contained in the star gates that were used to cement Earth with life, Humanity will find itself integrating the new paradigm shift at levels of the psyche.

Communication forms will ascend and those beings you think can't speak, will be the ones who without doubt, serve as the golden communicators between the councils of other dimensions and that of Earth.

Many things will be shifting still on E as the poles too, re arrange themselves towards the poles of Tara[15], Gaia[16] and Aramatena[17].

Once this 4-year adjustment period, with human time takes place, the portals of intergalactic communication will be open for higher conscious beings.

Many lies shall be revealed from those in the power status on Earth.

The Truth, as we have stated for eons, shall set all free.

---

[14] A cluster star system in our Milky Way galaxy, also known as the seven sisters, it is the nearest of all-star clusters and visible to the naked eye. It is in the Taurus constellation. www.urbandictionary.com

[15] Planet counterpart of Earth in dimensions 4-5-6

[16] Planet counterpart of Earth in dimensions 7-8-9

[17] Planet counterpart of Earth in dimensions 10-11-12

Message 4
The Cosmos,
By Lord Matreya

August 29, 2012 - 9:01 PM

What the DNA of the body is to man,
the cosmos is to the gestalt of luminaries called God.

As the first opens up, just as the lotus would,
so it will be done by the cosmos, revealing to human beings mysterious places
that many have labeled as planets.

Humanity shall never perish, as it is encoded
with the essential frequency tone that elevates the universal spirit
towards its own embodiment as the divine itself.

As atoms would create life on many planes,
so it is that the human DNA will be intertwined with the strands
of illuminated wisdom.

As stated it is spoken, and as spoken it is done.

Message 5
By Lord Matreya

August 29, 2012 - 9:03 PM

The circulatory system of Earth will flood out
what many will call diseases, fabricated by men itself
based on their lack of wisdom and a PHD on ignorance.

The rivers and oceans will respond accordingly,
through the cleanse that will take place,
thou shall not despair as absolute protection is given
for those choosing to vibrate the higher hertz frequencies.

Use the voice
Use the color
Use the form
Earth shall heal
and so shall thou.

Message 6
By Sri Babaji Nagaraj

August 29, 2012 - 9:06 PM

*The stars sisters will move,
the belt of Orion[18] will open.*

*The hidden beings in places of power
shall reveal themselves in the year 2015.*

*I shall not give prophecies but a view of the future
created by the collective universal consciousness.*

*Just remember this,
Love will still be, is and will always be
the ultimate power that transcends life itself.*

*Immortality is hidden in this experience,
and not for another.
Not emotional love that attaches itself to form,
but the love that emanates from within,
where all is created and destroyed.*

*As nothingness speaks, the everything births itself.
Such is the power of love.*

Remain in it, and fear shall be no more.

---

[18] The belt of Orion is a pattern of some of the most famous stars in the night sky, in the constellation Orion. It consists of the three bright stars: Alnitak, Alnilam and Mintaka. www.universetoday.com

Message 9
By Brother Issa

August 29, 2012 - 9:15 PM

The Book of Revelation[19] has been distorted.

*Yet no more in hidden frequencies that locked
the matrix in a repetitive program.*

*Random choices repeating themselves,
to distribute a false sense of variety.*

Nothing has been diverse, all has been one and the same.

The truth about my passing will be revealed.

I died not.

*I crucified myself not
inserted has been my story.*

I have not even been on Earth.

---

19 The *Book of Revelation*, and full name being *St. John's Revelation*. This last book of the Bible describes visions and a "Revelation" seen by St. John in which he goes to Heaven. This book illustrates the second coming of Jesus Christ to bring his children to Heaven. www.urbandictionary.com

Message 10
By The Council of AH

August 29, 2012 - 9:22 PM

*The divine trinity will be born, in flesh and bones
for the first time as the month of the frequency 11 takes place.*

*The being is a God creator, which will bring the new glad tidings
to the next civilization.*

*A new Euiago cycle shall begin; the new codes emerging
As the new tools of healing the "all".
Humanity will take back its power.*

An intergalactic battle will not affect the happenings of the human spirit.

*The creation experiment has been a success.
Humans are ready to create their own universe
as we all in the galaxy ascend.*

*We recognize the power of this gestalt called humanity.
The Tri-Vecas,[20] shaped as the human heart
will burst open as the hidden keys for ascension are unlocked and revealed.*

*The new emissaries will descend.
A massive amount of people will ascend.*

*And during the next 4 years after the cycle of the solar prophecy takes place,
we all shall return to pay the necessary tribute to Earth,
as the seeding process will have had its rightful harvest.*

The second seeding will take place not on Tara, nor on Earth, but in AH.

---

[20] An image, formed by 3 circles representing a specific mathematical program.

Message 11
By St Germaine

August 30, 2012 - 8:28 PM

*The waters of Earth will divide themselves
as the emotional stream of consciousness itself
changes on Earth.*

*The restoration of values, this takes place effortlessly
after much needed awakening of the human heart
in to what truly matters.*

*The moon will rotate its sphere towards balance,
the sun will eclipse the moon 12 more times and thus with this
announce the new era and the opening of holographic portals
closed to the ordinary eye.*

*The Violet Flame[21] power will descend, as it shall be the tool of truth
that shall be spoken, through the telepathic intent of the chosen ones.*

---

[21] The Violet Flame is one of the greatest little-known spiritual tools on the planet, and a tremendous gift from God to mankind. It's an aspect of God's light and energy, also known as the Flame of Forgiveness or the Mercy Flame. Violet fire has the power to transmute negative karma - this means to change the burdens of negative energy that we have accumulated through the ages into positive energy. We feel lighter, happier and we don't have to suffer through so many of the 'bad' aspects of life. www.spiritual-encyclopedia.com

Message 12
By The Council of AH

August 30, 2012 - 8:34 PM

*The vortex of the human spirit will be open
the veils of separation shall fall.*

*The ones that carry the keys.
The ancient ascended ones left on Earth,
shall one by one ascend
creating the path that many shall follow
towards their own magnificence.*

*Will power shall transmute I to the voice of the ones
that will earn the right to led Earth.*

*The systems that have no foundations of spirit shall fall,
the abuse of power extinct.*

*Generations to come shall rejoice once the integration process
has come to completion.
Golden beings will give support to the Indigo[22] children,
who tired of the journey, will have received their earned gifts.*

*The children shall assist no longer to the jails of schools,
the new era shall begin.*

---

[22] It is said that the Indigo children are born with 3 DNA strands activated instead of 2. Their purpose on the planet is to raise their consciousness and to support humanity ascend.

Commentary On Part I
The Universal Awakening

Once the soul awakens, the search begins and you can never go back.
~ John O'Donohue

For me, the first step in this awakening process was to ask myself, *What is truth and what is real?* What if the crucifixion of Jesus was indeed a movie inserted in this matrix system, an illusion created to hold control over the human family's mind and behavior? Or, what about the statement that the human race was seeded on earth? Does that mean that the (his) story of human kind's evolution theories are all illusions as well? What if "time" indeed is nothing more than a program to hold humanity in a well structured matrix?

I was positively surprised by how much the Ascended Masters revealed; specific dates and events are clearly mentioned. All that is stated in the messages make sense to me; the restoration of higher values in thoughts, words and acts, the awareness that what we provide our body with will smooth the transition of change so that my body can align to higher cosmic vibrations.

Reading this first part I heard the wake up call to pull the plug out of ancient installed programs in this matrix system. A system, which appears to be a mental prison of ignorance where programs, called live experiences, are repeated randomly. I reviewed movies such as *The Matrix*, and *The Truman Show* with another awareness. I am aware that there are many movies, books, and speakers revealing parts of reality, and I do realize that it depends the level of consciousness and mindset how each individual chooses to perceive the message embedded within them.

I experience that ascension is not about leaving my body. I ascend with my body into higher consciousness. With this readiness I continued my journey with an open mind through this portal with my awareness *unplugged!*

And with this awareness I invite you to start the next part.

PART II
THE DEATH OF POLITICS

Message 13
By Lord Matreya

August 31, 2012 - 10:23 PM

*The patterns of the matrix will reveal themselves
as faulty systems take place.*

*Earth as it is known is non-existing.
The projected holographic insertions*[23] *will fail
as Saturn and the moon collapse as a meteorite hits the 3rd ring
which transmits the necessary holograms that keep Earth in its place.*

*The systems of power shall collapse with this.
The rulerships or presidencies will take a new walk.
Women shall reign,
reptilian forces be discovered
and all just as the last programs of a matrix that was intended
to work until December 23rd of 2012 time frame Earth.*

*The new constitutions shall be given
to the new founder-races.
As hybrid forces wrote the books that keep humanity
in subconscious captivity
and the power of the female stagnated in hormonal waves.*

*Thus as this program completes, the races shall gather again
to determine the next evolutionary process,
beyond the system that works no more.*

---

[23] Insertions (images) made of holograms

Message 14
By Master Kybalion

August 31, 2012 - 10:29 PM

The night shall present its gifts to the deteriorated minds.
The obscure darkness will receive a new opportunity.
The necessary changes take place
rearranging the system,
the program.
Few will break free the training completed,
sent to the higher universes to protect the essence of the divine.

The background and pure transmission
that creates the whole and everything;
the alchemist,
the golden liquid realms.

Those who rule must do so in humbleness.
This is the frequency that gets the masses
out of the followership phenomena.

Awaken like the mountains will
envision like a Michelangelo or a da Vinci.

The 144000 shall travel back home
and activate the avatar genome through the av1 activation.
It is time.

Message 15
By Kwan Yin

August 31, 2012 - 10:37 PM

Thousands of years the humanity you all have experienced has been, but walking blind, in a path of pre-conceived reality.

Nothing new, all repeating itself over and over.
Experiments of the conscious mind
trying to experience itself in its full diversity
setting up the stage for what thousand universes experience.
Sending its creatures
its crawlers
its mammals
to an environment where life is the main goal.

The Death star, shall return to the orbit of the galaxy
and the black box of the matrix will crack open
by the release of trapped souls who think they must have a body.

The restoration of the vessel for human souls will shift
many shape shifters revealed.

Queens, and castles astonishing the world by their particular
genes of transmutation and bio-regenesis powers.
Monarchies shall disappear
the new reign is for the awakened ones.

Earth will go through a soul cleansing
a restoration of human consciousness.

Message 16
By Sri Babaji Nagaraj

August 31, 2012 - 10:45 PM

*An atomic bomb of revelations will collapse the hidden agendas
of the dictators of Earth.
Those whom genocide seems to be a population control system.
Those who release diseases just for the sake of power,
claiming that viruses that are new are discovered.*

Nonsense!

*The truth is that the operating system that holds the illusory
in place is falling apart.
The portal of awakening is taking place.
The founder races, protectors of Earth are coming back to rescue
and take with them those who came to support humanity to ascend.*

*Humanity SHALL NOT PERISH.
An intergalactic war has taken place for eons regarding this.
Races of beings disapprove.
They see humans as a compromised program that can spread its viruses to other systems*

*Faith has been a tool that has kept the frequencies going and restoring.
The reboot will take place.
Time and poles will readjust.*

Women will take back their power.

Message 17
By Sri Babaji Nagaraj

August 31, 2012 - 10:57 PM

Inter Stellar vibrations and frequencies will be off tune.

Those who know about hertz, color, and sound will have an advantage.

The houses of power will try to diminish the effectiveness
of these methods which have been passed by the higher ancestors
to those who will become the greatest healers.

Medication as humans know it must disappear,
it is the micro
it is the sound
it is the essences
the shape and colors, which will regenerate the cell of immortality
and advance civilization to an individuated era.

Listen well.

Message 18
By Lord Matreya

September 1, 2012 - 9:51 PM

*The eye rhythm and patterns of the human face
are synchronized with programs on what many call the media.*

*The way the broadcasting of information works, through the influence
of the political structures and the hands that hold the power over humanity,
is created in a way that the eye rapid movement is like a masterful dance
where it moves where it has to in order to program subconsciously the messages,
commands and instructions of obedience that are sent through what you call
entertainment, news of fear and the structure of inserts called wars.*

*Many will start to awaken upon this matter,
and matter shall be no more considered as such.
The waters that rise are generated by machines.
The climate controlled by precise holodynamic[24] gravity powers.*

*The reptilian kings and queens that hold earth as its hostage shall begin
the decline of their empires.
The places where all money is held shall be revealed.*

*The truth shall set you free and nothing shall remain in the veils of the hidden
and when we say nothing, we meant nothing.*

---

[24] Holodynamics views reality as a coherent, dynamic, living, holographic information system whose structure, from micro (smallness) to macro (bigness) is intimately connected with human consciousness. Consciousness is considered a prime condition of the holodynamic universe. It is not limited to a single space-time continuum but emerges from parallel dimensions into a coherent potential for each individual (the fully potentialized self). This personal potential manifests as a quantum potential field within the microtubules of every living cell of the human body and underlies all bodily functions including mental and social functions. Source: http://www.holodynamics.com/

Message 19
By Kwan Yin

September 1, 2012 - 9:59 PM

Voting is a joke in your humanity.
What to vote for? And whom to vote what?
Words paradoxically used for what humanity considers as diversity.

Wake Up!
Can't you see that the many that you think you are to choose are one of the same? Programmed and marked with the lines of those who have been precisely prepared to become the puppet of perfection for the master puppeteers.

I say this on to thee, thy consciousness will set thee free and protect thee from being seen.

Like the Itzaes[25] did, the powers of invisibility of thy energy vibration can and must be veiled.

Learn the skills of the alchemists
as you watch what many call horrors dissolve, when your consciousness cannot retain neither contain the perpetuation of pain neither its existence.
The veils lift.
The lies fade.
Awakening is the target.

---

[25] The Itza are the founders of Chichen Itza Maya, its capital par excellence. In Maya Itza means "water witch," a term that comes from the worship of water that existed in this city, geographically located in the Mexican state of Yucatan. In pre-Hispanic times it was the most famous cenote, where they carried out the rituals, sacrifices, dedicated to the water deities. centzuntli.blogspot.com/2011/05/itzaes.html

Message 20
By Sri Babaji Nagaraj

September 2, 2012 - 7:41 PM

*Micro chips of information installed in the blood fluid of those
who have mastered the use of words, not to empower, neither to motivate,
but program in the mind of their followers, promises, hopes,
and aspirations that are futile.*

*Enlightenment is a sweetened program, so it is sex, compassion, kindness
and love.
Do not misunderstand as we do honor the greatest frequency on the universe
as love itself.
Not a love that contains a how, a when or a meaning,
but a love that transcends time and source as it ascends the same essence of
its creator.
However the love that your humanity abuse, sell, and advertise,
it´s based on the conditioned.*

*And this, shall be removed
and the women will awake.
And as this takes place the men will buy not, nor sell, that which distracts the
human soul from its mission;
the ascension of the universal mind.*

Message 21
By Sri Babaji Nagaraj

September 4, 2012 - 8:50 PM

As the new rulers shed their skin, reptilian colors shall emerge.
All families of the same nest,
leaving eggs of reproduction and programming beyond what
the ordinary mind can grasp.

Few unplug from the matrix, those few will share their awakening massively.
Few unplugged before
they ascended in stellar ships called star gates.

This shall happen again.
Raise thy frequency.
Surround thyself by higher foods, higher beings, and thoughts of present presence.

And out of the matrix thou shall be, right now, here and now.

Message 22
By Babaji Nagaraj

September 4, 2012 - 8:53 PM

The signpost of a true master will not be its intricate, complicated teachings, or its sales of simplicity, neither sophistication nor the ability to sit down breathing for days without eating.

No! this era is the era of the awakened ones who choose words as mathematical tools.
The fallen have used these as weapons. Reverse this by using them wisely.

Awaken the word, and you unplug humanity in a collective way.

On December 23rd 2012 the gateway for this will be open, will remain open for exactly 244 human days.

Get ready, choose thy words, and create with them the Merkabahs[26] that will ascend thee beyond the mind and into the experience of beings that met the divine face to face within.

Rise!

---

[26] Merkabah, also spelled Merkaba, is the divine light vehicle allegedly used by ascended masters to connect with and reach those in tune with the higher realms. "Mer" means Light. "Ka" means Spirit. "Ba" means Body. Mer-Ka-Ba means the spirit/body surrounded by counter-rotating fields of light, (wheels within wheels), spirals of energy as in DNA, which transports spirit/body from one dimension to another. www.crystalinks.com

Commentary On Part II
The Death Of Politics

I was really too honest a man to be a politician and live.
~ Socrates

I sense that the changes we are to experience in the political world are enormous. I can imagine genetic families, groups including pharmaceutical industries, religious institutions, banks, justice systems and media that have exercised control for many centuries will step off their thrones and be replaced by feminine energy in the form of highest values of humbleness, kindness, compassion and guiding by modeling.

During the weeks of the transmission of the messages, I did more research on these topics than I had done during the previous fifteen years and followed my intuition on what I consider as truth.

Being part of this collective consciousness, I do have memories from other lifetimes stored in my cells about religious beliefs and the different organizations. As I have not been raised with particular data from religious institutions in this lifetime, I did my research on ancient texts with a complete open mind. For some reason, one day out of nowhere, the Book of Revelations and the Hermetic Teachings of the Kybalion appeared on my computer.

On August 31st all day I literally heard sounds and specific tones, which I could not understand nor give a place to at that moment. At night message seventeen arrived informing us that hertz frequencies, color and sound are tools to regenerate the human cells. I instantly thought of the Codes of AH, created by Ivonne, which are such tools. They are infused with sounds, mantras, color and sacred geometry. I love co-creating with these codes and support myself as well as others in increasing self awareness and self healing.

I consider this chapter also a call to remind ourselves that ascending our global consciousness is what we are to focus on. Moreover, it is a call not to get emotionally distracted by upcoming events or revelations related to humanity or other life forms.. I see the changes as positive and with joy! I strongly believe in the good.

Sri Babaji states firmly: Humanity shall not perish. – I choose to believe this and I am reminded of a conversation I was having with him 3 years ago where I shared that the vision of the future immediately projects a happy face on my inner screen: I see happy children playing and laughing. We remained in silence for a while and then he asked me to hold that vision. I still do today! A very simple practice of how to create a reality – something that is within the power of what each of us can do.

The masters give us a powerful tool for unplugging collectively from the matrix, "to awaken the word and use it wisely." I don't take it for granted, and I decided to be even more mindful than before of my thoughts and words.

Now let us explore what the next part is revealing!

PART III
RECONNECTION WITH EARTH

Message 23
By Kwan Yin

September 4, 2012 - 8:59 PM

The electromagnetic fields on Earth are designed to keep humanity plugged to the source of the matrix.

It is considerate enough as an act of common sense, soul wisdom to unplug all artificial energy deliverers, and plug thyself into nature as it contains the wisdom to support thee for ascension transcendence and more.

Listen to the frequencies that matter and use technology wisely.

Remove thyself from it if thou are automatized and have become a slave of it.

Carry the Vogel[27] technology with thee.

Be prepared.

---

[27] Marcel Joseph Vogel (1917 - 1991) was a research scientist. He received numerous patents for his inventions during this time. Among these was the magnetic coating for the 24" hard disc drive systems still in use. His areas of expertise were phosphor technology, liquid crystal systems, luminescence, and magnetics. In the 1970's Marcel did pioneering work in man-plant communication experiments. This led him to the study of quartz crystals and the creation of a faceted crystal that is now known as the Vogel-cut® crystal. The Vogel-cut® crystal is an instrument that serves to store, amplify, convert, and cohere subtle energies. www.vogelcrystals.net

Message 24
By Lady Nada

September 4, 2012 - 9:53 PM

Inner Earth is awakening
the beings of the undergrounds shall rise.
Despair not as earth shakes
the Californians.
The grids align.
The light of night will keep radiating the disturbing energies
that keep women dormant and lead them astray.

Yet, on the day 12, of the month 8, of the year 13, this shall stop.

The power of she will rise, with the oceans.
As the satellite that sustains the matrix, shall be deactivated
by beings from AH.
With full support of moon soul beings.

I have spoken.

Message 25
By The Council of AH

September 4, 2012 - 9:56 PM

The revolution against GMO's[28] will begin and this is a sign for all AH BEINGS to prepare for the crusade.

Gather thy families and tools.
Begin to raise the frequency and focus on the values you are encoded with.
As thee are the ones that will get the beings out of the dissolved Earth Matrix.

Begin now:
80% raw foods.
Wintertime do as the Indians do.

Be prepared.

Thou are the keys that will move the star gates forward.

---

[28] Genetically modified organism.

Message 26
By The Council of AH

September 4, 2012 - 10:01 PM

The sun is an emissary of AH.
Eons of attacks have no power over this soul energy field
where the gestalt of ascended ones collide as one.

The reign of fear is over
and the sun has an agreement to let his golden children out of Earth.

They will bring the 144000 that were chosen to participate
in the new EARTH beginnings.

As the reconnection and healing of Earth and Tara happens
a new Earth shall be created.

The Golden Tara, the one that lives behind the Pleiades
and that has been veiled until now.

Message 27
By Lord Matreya

September 4, 2012 - 10:13 PM

The Four Suns (and the hertz 676, 364, 312, 676)
shall begin vibrating
when the end of the cycle begins.

The eyes that see will see the whole of realities.

The orbs shall bring down the white man
from dimensions four, six and seven
numbers, numbers, numbers
unblocked the reality of fanaticism.

Drop the need to obey.
Its time!

Rebel in peace.
Aho!

Message 28
By St Germaine

September 4, 2012 - 10:19 PM

How many particles of light are required for humanity to willingly drop the veils of separation?

We have worked for eons and this has been only a fragment of creation.

The guardians of the sacred codes from the different god creator races:
Indigos
Crystal
Golden Beings from AH
and the Violet Gestalt team
gathered at once in centers of earth where awakening takes place.
Prepare the new temples of initiation as the sacred number align with 12
77
99
and 1111
Thus earth shall open its gifts of wisdom to thee.

This is the call from beyond thou have been longing for.

Message 29
By Master Ebeelon

September 7, 2012 - 7:10 PM

*Those whose words are used for defense strategies,
their own words shall turn into self weapons.*

*Any male that uses words or force
to violate the safety of the sacred feminine,
these would be his self chosen weapons against his soul.*

*Words are mathematical structures,
used wisely they unlock unlimited potential.
Used ignorantly, while pretending to be enlightened,
have the harmful force of an atomic bomb.*

*Yet words have more power than neutrons and atoms.
DNA responds to them, not words to DNA.*

*Perception creates reality.
Choose wisely.*

I have spoken.

Message 30
By Sri Mataji

September 7, 2012 - 7:12 PM

When the oceans rise, is a sign
that the waters of spirit have been suppressed.

Deny not emotions,
neither the mind.
Support tools are these.

Decompress and deprogram
what the matrix has installed in thee.

Open thy heart literally with the power of imagery
and unlock what is hidden and untouched from those
who seek to create a flock of herds of humanity.

Awaken.
Let the sun warmth in.
Say AH!

Message 31
By Hilarion

September 7, 2012 - 7:13 PM

Rise thy thoughts and praise the earth below you,
the sky above you,
the fire inside of you
and the water that runs through you.

Rise and praise every moment of transcendence,
the Earth as the spirit matter of the divine feminine.
Praise the masculine.

If thou seek to prove thy truth, thy truth will disappear.

Thou are not a name,
a label,
or a machine.

Thou are a sacred code called human being.

Message 32
By Lord Kuthumi

September 7, 2012 - 7:16 PM

*Open the particles of higher values
and you will find the emissaries
of the Council on Earth.*

*They have been tattooed with a power
to serve like no other.
They have skills of organization and productivity
like no one does.*

*They serve their families,
their communities
the world.*

*They create,
they are proactive,
they speak,
they revel.*

*They are the golden beings to support Earth
and the masters that are veiled by their ego
in Earths awakening process.*

AHU!

Message 33
By St Germaine

September 7, 2012 - 9:26 PM

*Each hemisphere is but a muscle
that can be isolated per will.*

*Use the 100 percent potential by approaching
the next visual.*

*Every morning, upon rising state the command
"Brain I shall train thee to obey!"
Visualize both hemispheres being filled
with golden liquid light.*

*Next, depending on the task ahead, command either
the left or right brain to function appropriately.
Give it the executive decisions.*

*When needed both hemispheres,
command the golden light to fill them both.
This deletes past imprints and memories
that belong to and feed the matrix, yet are not yours.*

*MEDITATE WITH A PURPOSE,
BEYOND PEACE, AND NO THOUGHT*

*Use this to master the mind.
Have a purpose!*

I have spoken.

Message 34
By Kwan Yin

September 7, 2012 - 9:30 PM

*Raise the feminine energy in ways that no force of
dark matter can ever create slavery of it again.*

*Use the visual of the rose.
See it unfold its petals in the heart chakra.*

*Simultaneously use a rose unfolding at the crown chakra.
Simultaneously see the stem of a rose with thorns
enveloping the radiance of thy soul.
These are not thorns of attack or defense but of protection.
Is a warning sign for intruders and systems.
If they choose to approach they will be dismantled.*

RISE WOMAN, RISE!

Message 35
By Sri Babaji Nagaraj

September 7, 2012 - 9:32 PM

Look to the cosmos.
What do you see?
Lights that shine as stars?
Have you believed everything
you have been told?

Well, it is time to wake up!
The holodynes,[29]
the holograms
are about to disappear.
And what shall thou do next without a support
and structure for a suppressive belief system?

Right!
Thou shall feel like falling,
however thou would be in reality ascending.

See this now
and come as you are.

---

[29] The physical manifestation or imprint of a living thought as it appears on an individual cell. www.urbandictionary.com

Message 36
By Brother Issa

September 7, 2012 - 9:36 PM

*The souls in young forms are still free.
The matrix was not intended to program
the soul in the form of a child.*

*Thus the matrix attacked the system,
and created a holographic insert of adultship being terrible.*

*A program where mothers are slaves,
where fathers distract themselves by lack of priorities.*

*Oh all you souls if you hear this,
remember thy inner child.
The matrix has no power over it.
Only thy mind that grows old in the time matrix
but not in you.*

*Liberate the child
and thou shall be the kingdom of heaven.*

Message 37
By The Council of AH

September 7, 2012 - 9:41 PM

Vegan? Lawyer? Spiritual? Older?
Ah! all the trash that the matrix doesn't know
where to put it recycles it in the labels
you all assume as identities.

The wasted matter of dark based reality,
recycled over and over again as a feeding mechanism
of the operative system called E.G.O
Energize Gates of Oppression!

The program is easy to dismantle and it is
with the hidden activation of hertz frequencies of 528
1111
729
and 927

Master the use of time as well.
If you master it, the program won't master thee.

Learn from the AH beings.

Message 38
By Master Metatron

September 7, 2012 - 10:05 PM

*The awakening of the feminine
will awaken the feminine powers also in men.*

*Let go of your limited beliefs based in the program of matrix
called p.o.w.e.r.
PRESSURE-OPPRESS-WIN-EXECUTE-REACT*

*A sequence of algorithmic expressions
that impresses the layers of the dermis transmitters
and so the epigenetics of the human genome.*

*Do not misunderstand the feminine awakening.
With witness
the man shall rise and be rebirthed from it.*

*This time as an avatar,
not a mere mortal hero.*

Message 39
By Master Kybalion

September 7, 2012 - 10:08 PM

*Reboot is about to take place
from 23-12-12 to 11-22-2017.*

*Master the forces of the breath,
they will be thy food.*

*Master the focus of the mind that transcends
and transmutes even the smallest particle
into palaces or desired manifestations.*

*Meditate! The mind of the One connects with thy mind as the One.
Thus broadcasting the necessary information
for the divine blueprint that transcends name, form and space.*

Begin the reboot now.

Message 40
By Master Hilarion

September 7, 2012 - 10:18 PM

*As you unplug a natural detoxification
and system cleanse process begins to take place.*

*As the deletion of the unnecessary implants takes place,
the DNA unlocks the wisdom of the ancients
myriads of lights activating in each particle of light itself.*

*THE VIRUSES that spread shall be a reaction
of the matrix in panic alarm state.*

*Threats galore will arise.
Despair not!
These have no power.
Thou shall triumph.
Cleanse, detox and replenish.*

*Get in thy Merkabah
and get out of there now!*

Message 41
By Sri Babaji Nagaraj

September 10, 2012 - 9:53 PM

When the confused ones begin to see what is not in others,
they will begin to radiate thousands of particles of misconception around.

Call it the flu, call it polarities, the disease most feared is not the one thy humanity knows, but the one that fragments the soul into pieces.

The true masters will speak of wholeness, not of fallen.
They will support and give.
They will see beyond what is right or wrong,
the goodness of all manifestations.

They will radiate a love that only the ones that go to the higher levels of love.
A love that is not to see what I get.
A love that doesn't do for others only if they do on to me.
But a love that transcends the I or You, where the giving-ness merges
with the receiver and thus becoming the absolute embodiment
of Christ consciousness.

As the pieces of soul fragment, the spirit behind it all will rise and bring back to wholeness that which was called negative or darkness
the time of light has arrived
and the song of love shall be heard at last.

Message 42
By Sri Babaji Nagaraj

September 10, 2012 - 9:57 PM

Oh gophers, lost in seeking the dark to understand it.
Thou loose thy time by doing so.
No power resides in there.
No why will be answered.
No question stated.

That realm is the realm of the lifeless,
the limited,
the fixed.

The true death that no soul has come to meet.
As the body completes its educational stages
the soul shall move in to the next dimensions.
Thus liberating itself from the illusion of separation.
The secret.
The fear.
The control.

I speak to thee; member of the 144,000 family.

STOP THY NONSENSE, OPEN THY HEART,
STOP SEEING ENEMIES WHERE THERE ARE NONE,
AND RISE!

ASCENSION IS HERE AND NOW!

Message 43
By Kwan Yin

September 12, 2012 - 4:17 PM

Be outside of the matrix of the Cyber trap.
Walk in nature barefoot for 5 minutes of thy tool of time.
Salute the sun.
At night dream and meditate before sleep upon the word AH.

This will take you beyond the programmed concepts,
will liberate thy mind from remote influencing
from planets and other beings,

Stay in the now.
Breathe the Earth.
Bless thy food.
Come back to Nature.

Commentary On Part III
Reconnection With Earth

The Earth is your grandmother and mother, and she is sacred.
Every step that is taken upon her should be as a prayer.
~ Black Elk, Oglala Sioux

One of my teachers told me a long time ago to focus on earth and not on the sky. I now understand what he meant was a metaphor; stay connected with the Earth, she provides us everything we need to remain physically and mentally healthy. The grounding keeps us protected to not become distracted by imposed events and thought-forms. The sky, on the other hand represents the distracter and transmitter of radiation from radar, antennae, satellites and radioactivity, as well as polluted thoughts and words.

While I was contemplating who could give me more information about bonding with Earth, I perceived images related to the Native Americans. For me they represent that part of the human family who truly embody and live with the sacred gifts of nature. I particularly loved this statement written by a Hopi Elder[30]

Our DNA is made of the same DNA as the tree. The tree breathes what we exhale, when the tree exhales we need what the tree exhales, so we have a common destiny with the tree. We are all from the Earth and when the earth, the water and the atmosphere is corrupted then it will create it's own reaction, Mother is reacting. To me is not a negative thing to know that there will be great changes, it's not negative, it's evolution. When you look at evolution, it's time, nothing stays the same.

---

[30] The Hopi Indians, who live in the arid highlands of northern Arizona, have inhabited the same place for a millennium, far longer than any other people in North America. They are not only the oldest dwellers in this land but are considered by most other Indians to have a wisdom, a knowledge of things, beyond average comprehension. Peace-loving and knit tightly together by clan relationships, they are intensely spiritual and fiercely independent. Their all-pervading religion is a many stranded cord that unites them to their stark, and beautiful environment. www.hopi.org

For a long time I have been doing research in texts within different cultures on the significance of the numbers in message 28: completion of a cycle, the pyramids, the universe (December 21) and the Divine Mother (December 12). I interpret the numbers as a direction to December 2012.

Several messages included hertz frequency numbers. I asked support from Phil and Judy Lahaye, co-founders of the Maitri Order.[31] They have been studying the hertz frequencies for several years. I noticed that by not taking the numbers literally and by reading between the lines the messages became more clear for me. I remain focused mainly on the expansion of the heart (love) and being present in the moment.

One day Ivonne and I were driving in the car and discussing about the function and use of the right and left hemisphere of the brain. That night the message of St Germaine was received (33) with a simple though powerful exercise for the brain.

When I read message 34 from Kwan Yin, I heard drums playing and I imagined the heart of Mother Earth beating with excitement. This inspired me to offer a Transcendental Rebirthing event on the beach. During the event I experienced a very strong connection with Mother Earth as if my breath resonated with her breath. I felt that when women rise and embrace their feminine power with grace and reverence, Mother Earth will transmute her sadness into creativity, power and love. This powerful radiance will dissolve any shade standing in the way to create a harmonic environment for all.

I experience that the matrix has no power over my thoughts and acts when I am in a state of joy, when I enjoy freely jumping in the waves of the ocean. Since this chapter was received I go out in nature even more than before, away from the computers. I enjoy walking barefoot on the beach, listening to the sound of the ocean, feeling the warmth of the

---

[31] The Silver Violet Maitri Order is a sacred fellowship where service and friendship towards all beings is awakened and acknowledged, which consists of living with friendly thoughts, words and acts. www.maitriorder.com

sun and watching children modeling the state of joy by their purity in thought, word, playfulness and free spirit!

After remembering the connection with Mother Earth, are you ready to transform yourself into a higher evolved species?
When yes, then begin with Part IV now!

PART IV
TRANSITION AS A HIGHER EVOLVED SPECIES

Message 44
By Lord Matreya

September 12, 2012 - 10:43 PM

To enter the star gate where the ancient initiated ones
traveled 2012 years ago, thou must all prepare accordingly.

The greens of Earth contain higher frequency that allow the body
to reach a sublime state to master the skills of
body transmutation,
invisibility,
quantum leap,
and de-materialization of form to teleportation between dimensions.

Prepare by alkalizing thy human form as the shift evolutionary in
essence will change the pH of the red river that runs inside the human form.

As the moon ceases its time program, women shall return
to a regular cycle of connection with Earth.
No blood shall be there.
Enlightenment by the thousands taking place at once in that moment.

Reproduction will become now truly ascended birthing.
And women will rise in positions of power that
at the beginning of Earths bountiful cycle, they kept the balance
of the universal laws clear.

Male energy shall come front and ease its fist and woundful words.
The Earth shall open like the lotus would.
Be ready.
Learn how to breathe.

Message 45
By Grand Father Jaguar

September 12, 2012 - 10:50 PM

*In the shadow of the serpent the death stars are allowed
to access earth cycles of completion and announcement of the new
years of perfect chronometry about to complete.*

*Oh dear souls.
Guard thy thoughts by meditation.
Guard thy tongue by presence language.
Guard thy actions by loving deeds.
Hide not thy shadow,
pretend not perfection.
For it is in vulnerable honesty that thou shall be granted
a space on the Merkabah for ascension.*

*The jaguar, the eagle, the serpent, the armadillo, the deer, the dance!
All gather in one fire,
one circle,
to receive the star souls that traveled before to be trained in the arts of ascension.
The ancient race shall return through the same portal they left.
Be ready!
On 12/13/12 they will select the ones that can guide others into the initiation
stages for resurrection of spirit.*

*The quetzal shall be back.
Tlaloc will pour songs of blessings.
And Xochitl shall pray for the children.*

*The brothers return.
The masters arrive.
The 144,000
A new constellation in the stars shall create.*

In'lackech

Message 46
By The Community at the Service of the Great Father of Sirius

September 12, 2012 - 10:59 PM

Brothers of the light,
The Brotherhood of the Universal Divine shows up once again
as a unique opportunity of creation.
Cry not!
Fear not!
For truth will lighten up your hearts.

I have danced eternally, and as I return I am ready to teach you
the simplicity of spirit,
the song of the stars.
And Mother Earth who will guide us to the knowledge of the new human existence.
Fear not!
Love!
Sing the song and feed your body only with happiness.

Do not try to emulate altered states of consciousness with alien substances.
It does not matter if they have been harvested in the earth.
Your inner seed is in your head.
The seed of creations contains it all.
Your heart contains the seed of the soul.

Children open your eyes.
Children open your arms.
Safety has been granted to you.
Fear not!
The guardians of the light are to arrive.

Message 47
By Cuathli Aguila Exche

September 12, 2012 - 11:04 PM

The calendar we have given to you is a code.
Open it, with caution and you will find the instructions
to travel through the soul portal.

We did not disappear;
we transcended.
We were taken by the cosmic field into an intergalactic travel
in which our big winged brothers signaled the way out.

We did not leave the matrix.
Yet, now that we are reuniting
with the other 144,000 we will achieve this.

We have not ceased to exist.
Various races desire what we have.
We travel without fear with the Brothers of the Jaguar families.
The emerald will guide your path.
The amethyst will heal your destiny.

Listen to the inner sound of the ball game.
The musical scale will play the 13th day of the month
you called the 12th, an awakening symphony.

10 days later, the equinox will bring the news
for the next stage.

Get away from those speaking about the fallen races.
Focus in your divine constellation family.

Message 48
By Kwan Yin

September 13, 2012 - 8:55 PM

*Pendulum like phenomena
embraceth circles that create the form of three.*

In the center thy intent shall birth itself powerfully.

*Drop the need to be acclaimed for thy deeds,
and then thy deeds shall be proclaimed by the universe.*

*Behold honesty and gentleness as the forces that are the same
as that of the ocean strength.*

*Behold the light of persistence, commitment and follow through,
the energies similar to the wind, the water and the fire.*

Embrace nature within.

Ascend humanity now.

Message 49
By The Ahu, Rah Gestalt

September 13, 2012 - 8:57 PM

Galactic brothers and sisters,
hear us well.
We are to support the transition in its stages of ascension.

The honor of the golden ones is shown in our sun
that welcomes thee all.

Technology shall be given freely to those who are ready
to transmute the DNA into liquid gold.

We are here!

And thus we accept the responsibility of supporting
thy planet and thy inner world.

Message 50
By Brother Issa

September 13, 2012 - 9:16 PM

*Thousands of years
waiting for this moment
to return to the place where I left once empty handed.*

*Leaving the technology of my realm in the hands of the races
that had hidden in their strategic plans the desire of destruction.
Experiment "earth-time" they called it.*

*We had to move fast.
We could not leave the golden, indigo, and blue luminaries seeds alone.
They sprouted soon enough for us to see that what we thought
was powerful, was even more powerful than expected.*

*Never before there had been experiments with soul wisdom.
The first stage of the observation process went well.
We arrived and the ones here already trained by the winged ones
were open to learn the mechanics of the laws.*

*We initiated them and attuned the scale of their soul
with the music of the spheres, a symphony of co creation.
Nevertheless,
the inner earth had sprouted too.
Reptilian forces coming from the stars.*

*I watched and saw that the laws were not respected.
It was I, and 12 ships with me, that we had to leave then.
We left behind 7 star gates
4 were damaged by the races
three were intact and hidden.*

*We implanted the counteracting program called LOVE,
as the races that wanted to dominate the new found field of life, Earth,
created the time matrix to keep humanity and the souls arriving
from galaxies beyond, imprisoned.*

*I ascended, as the brothers of the stars did.
We created a code.
Thousands of them.
Implanted them in the soul particles that were still free.*

*I was created as a program,
a hologram of myself implanted in humanity.
I watched patiently from above
as below was showing what was not truth.*

*It will be then, that on the time matrix
on the year 13 I shall return.*

*I come to restore the grids,
the star gates,
the DNA,
to restore the program of Love.*

*In it no time exists
the plasmic[32] field of fear disappears.*

I am One, I said this before.

I am the Son of God.

---

32 Adj from plasma. The clear, yellowish fluid portion of blood, lymph or intramuscular fluid in which cells are suspended. In physics: an electrically neutral, highly ionized gas composed of ions, electrons and neutral particles. Thefreedictionary.com

Message 51
By The White Brotherhood Gestalt

September 13, 2012 - 9:20 PM

*Brothers of the stars, brothers of the stars
hear us now
as we descend to take what is ours.*

*Do not run away in fear when you see us come.
Hidden nothing shall be unveiled.*

*We are the Brothers of the White.
We come as human forms as we once were human before.
We surrendered to the matrix in order to experience it
and came to know its mechanism.
When the contract was completed we exited to the 15 D.*

*However, it got also suppressed by the matrix that by now
has grown in its power by the energy of terror,
fear,
desistence,
and lack of will power.*

*Comfort is a program.
Thousands of our sent brothers give in to it.*

*They'd rather sleep than be awake.
They'd rather rest than serve.
We are coming back.
We will get the work done.*

*We shall ascend.
Earth, Tara, Gaia hear our call,
we are coming back to you.*

Message 52
By Abraham

September 13, 2012 - 9:29 PM

When the fetus is growing the battle begins
at the level of soul existence.
Thousands of billions of beings collide.
Battles over battles to access the entrance towards the matrix.
Many interested in planting their own programs there.
Others interested to come join their already imprinted armies.

Mind is dormant, thou must awaken it.
Soul battle is well seen in the reflection of the amphibians on Earth.
Sounds of the oceans unlock soul potential.
Hidden in the depths of the center.
There are thousands of races waiting for a turn.
They all desire to exit.
The matrix won't allow this,
as it feeds from conflict, fear, and control.

However, the happening of the projected time matrix will not take place.
The day of 12/21 and 22, and 23, and 24, and 25
an orchestrated projection screen
it will be just another ordinary day.
The portal opens up on 12-13 afterwards just watch
the theater of the fake scenarios of media:
Egypt
Giza
Afghanistan
Tel Aviv
Canada

*All distracters as the star gates are moved from places.
An army of telekinetic beings has been created already
by the governments of your planet.*

*We shall come, and like the ancient texts we left here, that are but codes of
instructions for exiting the matrix, we shall battle as well.*

*Read the Bhagavad Gita.
Speak the language of Sanskrit.
The most prefect language the matrix cannot decode.*

*Find it.
Attune with it.
Master the sound signature of thy voice.
Through it thy soul will ascend.*

Message 53
By Lord Kuthumi

September 13, 2012 - 9:34 PM

Count 108 carefully!
Add 2
Plus 400
Plus 2
Plus 44.
Those are the number of days that the matrix must be reprogrammed.

AFTERWARDS IT WILL LOCK OF ITSELF.

Count the steps to the palace.
Count the steps to the warrior temple
and count the columns on the wind portal.

Thus you have these days to reprogram Earth for peace.
You have three human years to reinstall the love program
activate it and ascend.

Then the matrix will lock itself.
It is a box,
decode it.
Use crystal wisdom.

Message 54
By Mary Magdalene

September 13, 2012 - 9:41 PM

Love was never an emotion.
It was a program I was sent to give to him
who carried the blame for all religious indoctrinations.
My beloved and I were assigned to take Earth to the level of ascended
soul energy wisdom.

Its DNA had to be activated ten thousand fold.
Its cells reproduced with clearer crystal silver linings.
I was seen as a threat for the races already here.
I was sent to activate the brain of man
and remove the reptilian implants on it.
I was never a program to fail.
I was created to activate and succeed
and with my beloved we created the love program.

It contains the energy hertz frequency that can restore Earth to its axis.
It can stop meteors from collapsing on earth.
It can heal the rivers.
It can summon the openings of the major channels of the universal mind
Thus we come back.
I have been here before now I write through me.

The program was polluted by the energy of the ultimate manifestation.
Sexuality was imprinted with reptilian phenomena
thus man gets lost in it.

Thinks it's for pleasure and reproduction when it is in truth
for creation of beams of light that will get the people
out of the linear to the non- linear experience.

Awaken now brothers and sisters.
Love each other as I have loved you.
Love thy neighbor as thy love thyself.
I spoke this, he spoke it to you.

It is time.
Welcome home.

Commentary On Part IV
Transition As A Higher Evolved Species

Be master of mind rather than mastered by mind.
~ Zen Proverb

While going through the integration of the messages in this book, it became more and more clear for me that these messages are direct transmissions from the highest realms without any infusion, interpretation of human emotions and/or implants. Only those who resonate with these frequencies can receive them. Ivonne can, as she is pure, humble and lives from the heart.

Specific dates are mentioned, and again it is stipulated that during the next 3 years we will enter a transition period. A transition to become "unplugged" from the matrix and to rise as a higher conscious species. These are such great reminders for me to not to get distracted and/or emotionally entangled in what the media will launch as major events in the near future.

Many of the messages were received from masters Ivonne and I did not recognize. We felt that the identity of the messenger was not to be confused with the message. Each message was an energetic transmission, beyond the name, beyond what we thought we knew of who the masters were.

One day Ivonne started receiving two messages directly in Spanish. These were the numbers forty-six and forty-seven. With this, the Spanish version of this book was born. Moreover, whatever the reason, upon message fifty-four while our physical bodies started the integration process of what we understood to be the final transmission the message came that the book was to continue… We both felt instantly that the book would be completed with 108 messages. And this is what happened.

This part of the book gave me the opportunity to contemplate on what makes a species more highly evolved. How is this higher evolved species thinking and acting? One thing is clear for me; A higher evolved species uses its own mind to think and not the mind of the matrix. Its' own free mind which is fed by healthy clean food provided by the earth and thoughts of honesty, elegance, commitment and higher awareness of truth and reality.

The desire grew to learn more about the *Love Program* Jesus and Mary Magdalene are writing about. The next part definitively gave me already some answers.
And I invite you to explore this for yourself.

PART V
UNPLUG PARENTAL PROGRAMS

Message 55
By St Germaine

September 18, 2012 - 9:31 PM

The light of reason shall illuminate the program called Parenting.
In truth it is a portal of transmutation and soul continuation.

Guardianship is granted to a soul that has come before another to experience Earth.
Many of these souls contain the wisdom that can liberate the thousands.

Do not lock thy mind in to believing children are thy own they aren't.
Serve them well.
Treat them with utter most respect.

The matrix won't plug them in if they but choose higher values as a way of loving.

The matrix is not built on reason and consciousness
It's built on fear.

Message 56
By Sri Babaji Nagaraj

September 18, 2012 - 9:58 PM

Fathers, oh fathers, set your mind at ease.
Reclaim the masculine power that you seem to have.
Yet is dormant by the numbness that the media has done upon thee.

Take care of thy beloved,
thy wife,
thy daughters.
Grow up!
Take care of thy family.

Embody the male energy which whole essence and presence
is benevolence, which creates the ultimate power.

The male paradigm lived until now is but a glitch
of the program of masculinity, as the matrix wants to control thee with its programs.

You are the master of masculine energy.
You are responsible of that side of the law of polarities, embrace it.
Masculine energy beyond the matrix has no violence on it.
It is filled with determination, ownership, certainty,
and absolute powerful loving care for thy family.

Don't get lost in the Maya.
The program that tells thee that in order to survive
thou have to compete with robots, automated beings that sell sex
sell stamina,
sell red luxury.

Awaken!
It is time.

Message 57
By Lord Kuthumi

September 18, 2012 - 10:30 PM

The process of selecting the guardians that thou call parents starts with a clear agreement between a member of thy higher soul tribe and thou.
Agreements upon mission, and contribution to universal awakening take place eons before soul process vibrates the necessary ionic combination of forces that propel the quantum field to generate the force that will make the soul travel through stellar cycles towards the matrix human.

An initiation takes place before embodying form.
The selection of parents is based by specific qualities and characteristics the soul desires to learn from in order to accomplish the mission.

Rarely the soul looks after the human history of the system
as the history of it is based on the matrix and not in reality.

Thus the process of conception takes place long before the child and the parents are even conceived.
When the necessary mathematical sequence is generated and the characteristics selected in the agreement collapse, the force of creation and expansion takes place.
Thus pulling in to the soul the necessary access towards the human matrix.
For this the selection process has been precisely selected by a binary method that has .000000000000000001 infinitesimal percentage of failure.

The exact time, the right geometry is met.
The soul descends when birth approaches.
Sometimes, rarely, depending on the evolved consciousness of the soul, it will access the womb matrix at the seventh gestational month on Earth.

This is but a first stage of 9 that takes place for human being creation. Thus this one refers to parental selection by the soul wisdom.

Message 58
By Kwan Yin

September 21, 2012 - 12:46 PM

*When a mother is born, thus the Earth begins the process
of downloading the necessary information for her to care for her offspring,
who will be hosting a higher soul at the same or higher vibratory rate
of those thoughts, actions and the legacies made by 12 generations past
of the combined ancestral imprints of both mother and father.*

*Thus the importance for a couple to prepare with meticulous focus before
the conception of the temple that will carry the offspring takes place.*

*The treatment the Mother receives is essential for the wellbeing
of the new being, that regardless of the age of the soul, will be arriving
to the divine feminine womb which is considered the temple of creation.*

*The environment around the mother and the love from the spouse is
essential for both mother and child be born in absolute harmony.*

*The more love and safety the mother feels, receives during pregnancy,
the less karmic ties and imprints the child will have.
Safety is a force field generator of ultimate purification.*

*Keep the mothers loved and safe and the new beings will radiate
this goodness for all in humanity.*

This is the way to birth an avatar.

Message 59
By Lord Matreya

September 1, 2012 - 12:20 AM

The father must go through a thorough purification process through body mind and spirit.
40 days this must be done.
Increasing his stamina by the right foods, the right exercise focus for the physical temple and the right mind supervision.
An intense inquiry of the mind must take place, to embody the ultimate protector for the family.

As the child is born, mother is born, and father is born for the first time.
Thus the divine trinity aspect of creation begins as the number 3 initiates a sacred mathematical equation that will generate necessary vibratory sequences to enhance the mission of all souls in the system.

Thus the father must be a warrior within, a battle against the matrix shall take place,
as the Maya program, distractions, fears, feelings of loosing freedom or identity begin to take place.
The boy must grow up, the teenager in him must be acknowledged, initiated and transmute the fire into purpose and passion, and birth the warrior that will provide in all realms for the mother and the child. His prize will be the love in return, the safety, the devotion the footprint of the next generations that will follow his lead.

In order to keep his mind out of the matrix, early rising must take place, early eagerness to live and work. Removal of all distractors that seduce the spirit into comfortability, creating handicapped souls trapped in the matrix field that sustains itself with this misalignment with source.

Every six months for 40 days the program must repeat.
Time alone the father must have.

Brotherhood he shall find.
Absolute commitment to his beloved and family a number one priority;
Letting go of his mother...and the desire to be cared for... his wife as a mother.
This will sustain him.

A man such is nurtured by forces beyond,
the universal laws align to him and within him.

All needed is delivered to the sound of AHO!

Message 60
By Lady Nada

October 1, 2012 - 10:40 PM

The vessel of human consciousness is particularly empowered by the universal laws through the parenting realm.

When a new being is born, ancient vibratory frequencies collapse and create what many would call an explosion of possibilities.

The Creator creates itself anew in the particle called human being, and it is able to share a soul fragment of itself through the embodiment of a unit called soul memory.

The quantum field radiates the necessary phenomena to attract the right circumstances in order for the materialization of form to succeed.
However, the programs enslaving parents are indeed inherited to the new soul via
the DNA, a transmitter that when reversed, it broadcasts exactly what the matrix desires to project as an apparent reality.
When activated in its full potential the DNA starts broadcasting the images of the reality that exist beyond the matrix and where conscious parenting which generates a love field space, takes place.

Whatever challenge you seem to have as a parent, awaken to the realization that full support is in thy way as long as you choose the L.O.V.E program. Patience is a skill that must be endured and peace of mind and of heart is the reward of what stillness brings into the play of consciousness.

Watch carefully your interactions, and your inner-actions, for as parents you become the puppeteers of the magnetic field where the new being will unfold, learn and develop.

Cut the cords of trying to control anything.
Drop all rules, become the master of thyself, cease the need to be loved and respected and these will take place effortlessly.

Remember to exit all fear-based programs by just setting the tone of thy mind in love.

The rest will take place by itself.

Message 61
By St Germaine

October 1, 2012 - 10:57 PM

The one being called THE ONE, in it has a thought trapped as a condensed thought vibration.
A grain of sand, a mustard seed is but the existence of a humanity that seems to see itself as small.
The grandeur of the human beings is that within them resides the power of ultimate alchemy.

Fathers and mothers receive this initiation as they receive a being in their guardianship either called son or daughter.
The skills of the magician and the goddess begin to be downloaded slowly as the time matrix allows it, so it won't collapse by the mega bytes of data that it contains.

An eradication of old programs must take place in order to receive the soul ware necessary to parent beyond the dogmas and the repetitive sequences of past labors of those who did not unplug.

The reason children pay the debts of parents is due to the fact that the program hasn't been deleted or upgraded. The belief systems, which are functions that transmit commands, when transferred verbatim from one generation to another, they repeat themselves exactly as they are.

A child however can break free of this conditioning by choosing different than the parents, and by activating the longing within to find the truth of who he is, which generates the necessary hertz vibrations to propel him to see reality in a multidimensional way.

Choice is a higher evolved command given to those who are willing to embark the journey to unplug the cord of illusion towards self-realization, Thus detaching and vibrating as a witness conscious of the programs, the *inheritances, the belief patterns and rising as a new being, as a new earth, as a new soul that finally will awaken and once and for all shall be born as a universal being, the primary and inevitable destiny of being human.*

Message 62
By Brother Isaiah

October 3, 2012 - 10:49 PM

To do what is right, is to merge in the realm of absolute mind mastery.
Thou shall use the tools and clues left in the metaphor world by the teachers before thee.

Word by word the transmission of the highest laws was given to the worthy ones,
the ones whose will power transcended the sin of doubt, judgment, and hesitation,
those who defeated the demons of believing in the idolatry of their ego or of other's ego.
The ones that rose above the turmoil of an un-ruled will.
Those who shook off the robe of delusion by conscious effort, hard work, committed patience, and service to others.
Those we call the worthy ones.
A shield of light surrounds their field, thus becoming invincible.

Parents thus have the opportunity of the embodiment of the art of worthiness by being absolutely present with one another and thus gift their children with this love.
The parents must command their whole being to treat kindly the young ones.
To use light touch, highest of respect of words, and model reverence of the ancestors they shall become if earned the title by righteous deeds.

Parents are not Patterns.
Unless they give in to the indulgences of the lower world where longing of outside wants and needs detour them from the sacred gift they have received of giving birth to the energy of life, and guiding it towards the reunion of the collective god head consciousness.

The tablets spoke the wisdom that would guide the parents precisely and completely.
The ancient masters shared their words.
Act upon them, not with words but with deeds.
As parents, liberate yourselves from the burden of repetitive heredity that replays itself when there is no aim or purpose pointed to divine love.

I have spoken brothers.

Message 63
By Buddha

October 4, 2012 - 9:30 PM

Consider this;

For a father to properly guide his daughters he must have absolutely respect, reverence and guardianship energy towards first their mother, then the children. Modeling with this to his daughter that the protection of the feminine energy is sacred.

For a Father to become the true leader of his sons, he must at all times show them how a warrior behaves. He must show them the proper care of the feminine, he must teach him the arts of farming and leadership. He must model with actions, not words, how to earn an honest living.

For a Mother to guide her daughter she must set aside her own needs and take nothing personal as the daughter grows and tries to find her own path. Support by nurturing must be present at all times and the mother must grow in elegance and character and assume her proper place, this will create a healthy luminous bonding.

The mother must show the grace of the feminine, the strength of purity, and the power of vulnerability. She must be the embodiment of absolute honesty, and the deliverer of the highest compassion skills only a Bodhidharma[33] can deliver.

At all times she must not behave as a father, and trust that the power of the ultimate Mother resides in her, thus she can relax and guide properly with firm clarity and benevolent wisdom.

---

[33] Bodhidharma, Chinese Putidamo, Japanese Daruma (flourished 6th century ce), Buddhist monk who, according to tradition, is credited with establishing the Zen branch of Mahayana Buddhism. www.britannica.com

For a mother, to guide her son she must know when the time comes, at age 13 or 14 the boy will be called for the stage of initiation. Before this, treat the child as the most gentle thing. After this, behold the man and allow the boy to grow.

Let go.

Message 64
By Ezekiel

October 4, 2012 - 9:44 PM

Oh such conceit it is the one of marriage.
Nevertheless, a concept indeed.

The truth is that as soon as a contract is made,
it is set in the stone of the Templars
that radiates the frequency of 528 hertz.
Radiating from the vessel that many call the sacred chalice[34]

The sacred glyphs[35] open their divination,
the mountains sing a song of praise.

A union of man and woman, a couple born from the program of love,
must remain working on accelerating its own consciousness as a one unit.

Whenever there is a betrayal,
a detour,
a disobedience of the laws, via man with other women,
or the woman distracted through contempt and subduing
her power for seduction only.

Thus then the sacred waters of the mother cease to bathe the union
and thus a trial time appears as they must prove themselves worthy
to receive the ultimate gift of their union,

---

[34] The Sacred Chalice is the physical container into which the Divine can enter and be held. In other words, it is a channel for Divine Energy and Consciousness. And *you* are this channel. It is your body and your mind, which need to be able to contain this Energy. www.wicca-spirituality.com

[35] 1: an ornamental vertical groove especially in a Doric frieze. 2: a symbolic figure or a character (as in the Mayan system of writing) usually incised or carved in relief. 3: a symbol (as a curved arrow on a road sign) that conveys information nonverbally. www.merriam-webster.com

*they meet
face to face
with God.*

Message 65
By Abraham

October 4, 2012 - 9:49 PM

Teach them well.
Hear this and this shall free you.

Liberation for all children of Earth is possible.
The stones spoke of it.

The laws were given
one by one counting 20
and then 20 more
and then 14 more.
144 families this was spoken to
just a few listened
even fewer were ready.

The light of Mount Sinai
radiated the glowing light of the silver orb
where the creator descended upon Earth
to deliver its assignments.

A test, a dictation
a proof that the laws of the universe have been in place
long before the One existed.

Attraction, alchemy, condensation.
The first three laws that must be spoken and be taught to a child.

Hear this well, as I walked my brothers out of danger
and got them closer to God.
Bring your children face to face with the luminous,
the sentient radiance of the portal of creation.

Sing songs of prayer,
chant the ancient sacred words
do the sound AH as my name bestows it.

I am Abraham, I am the son of God.

Message 66
By Brother Issa

October 5, 2012 - 9:17 PM

*The one thing that will be and is
the most important teaching to give to the children
in a family system is this:*

*Love is indeed the ultimate power.
The heart is the highest chakra,
is the center of being that radiates the waves
that connects the earth with higher heavens.*

*The air thy breathe is the air that will recreate
life over and over again.
Air evolves, love evolves.
The highest chakra is at the center of being.
It generates the lead
the light
come back to it when feeling lost.*

*Nothing dies.
Your light, thy soul
is immortal.*

*Death is a pause of review.
A cleanse, a detox program from what was experienced as non-real.*

*Fear not the end, nor the beginning.
For thy love,
thy children,
thy couple-ship,
thy family,
thyself,
is love.*

Commentary On Part V
Unplug Parental Programs

*Your children are not your children, they come through you,
but they are life itself, wanting to express itself.*
~ Wayne Dyer

The Masters mention that from the moment parents meet or what we call "fall in love" their mission frequencies are increased. I reconsidered my own journey from child to adult, then as a spouse and mother, and my personal awakening process over the past few years. I am grateful for the great teachers on my path. Family members and partners, friends, mentors and professional relationships, many of them holding up a mirror, offering me an opportunity to gaze – at my own reflection.

Conception takes place long before the child and the parents are conceived, states Lord Kuthumi in message fifty-seven. This reminded me the saying of Mark Wolynn[36] during a family constellation training that *when our grandmother was born we were already in her womb*. At that time I did not really paid attention to this remark. Yet, now it makes total sense to me.

I understand that besides being born with inherited patterns, which are transmitted through our DNA from parents and ancestors, we also come with our own individuated qualities to learn related to our own soul mission and agreements made long before even our parents are conceived. Having given birth to and being a mother of a beautiful daughter, a radiant soul of greatness, I now consider with even more humbleness than before the joy, honor and privilege she chose me to be her mother. The messages are beautiful. It is truly a guide from a to z for the parents of the world. When followed I can imagine living in a society surrounded only by loving and conscious families.

---

[36] Mark Wolynn is the Director of The Hellinger Institute of Western Pennsylvania, Northern California and the Co-Director of The Hellinger Learning Center in NYC. He conducts workshops and trainings in family systems therapy all over the world. www.hellingerpa.com

Kwan Yin names that safety is a force field generator of ultimate purification. I love this one! For years I did not really understand what the feeling "safety" meant until I was guided by Ivonne, a true advocate for the children, in my very first Transcendental Rebirthing experience. The manifestation of the past missing childhood experience of safety created an instant change in my present adult energetic field. This experience not only led me to become a Transcendental Rebirthing trainer myself and rebirth adults, though also to become a Doula (birth attendant) with the aim to provide an environment of absolutely safety for the mother while giving birth to her baby.

What a great opportunity the Masters gift us with how to unplug parental programs with wisdom never revealed before in such clarity. This wisdom will accompany you in the next Part where the keys of Enlightenment are clearly exposed.

PART VI
ENLIGHTENMENT

Message 67
By MA

October 6, 2012 - 8:44 AM

To contribute is the highest state and mark of the illuminated being.
A master indeed he /she is who as well, raises up in the morning
eager to work and serve.
Hidden lurking thoughts of comfort, wanting to sleep and still at the same time wanting to manifest unlimited abundance, will not manifest as congruency, an essential quality of the master.

The master is willing to set aside his own needs for the needs of others.
He has an uncanny ability to say yes and a mastery in productivity like no other being.
He is awake, ready to teach, serve and learn.
He has tapped into a resource of energy that few know about.
Her willingness to show up
to feed the souls of others with creativity raises the master above the mundane while humility grows beyond time.

She remains steady and focused.
He remains calm and centered.
The master is beyond sex and ideas.
He treats all opportunities with kindness.
He drops the need to be right and allows the range of emotions
to be stilled like an ocean will,
or unleashes their power when in need to awaken others.

The master produces unlimited wisdom, and is creative like no other being on Earth. She can answer all questions, write the sacred texts of all wisdoms, and think beyond the box of pettiness, of a delusory realm, which seems real yet is not.

A master is the ultimate alchemist.
He will know when to open up the wound of comfortability in others in order to allow its healing.
The master is active outside, passive inside.
Those who desire the attainment of enlightenment,
yet have become slaves of work, of time and complaint about it.
Who use vocabulary as "I have to" they will never find this portal.
Those who know they are the masters of themselves,
who can let go of the needs of the world and reconnect with nature.
To him belongs the kingdom and wisdom of the ancients.

Rules kill the master, flexibility awakens him.

Parasitical strategies of others to get enlightened, or get rich, on, or in his/her behalf, soon are revealed as wounds, as pain, as suffering.
For the master knows he is but a student of these beings, that walk close to him to get his ideas, that remain close to her to achieve success, that want what the master has yet want little effort or work to do.

The master knows this, and in the right timing, he lets go of these students, as part of his own reflection of his own thoughts.

Thus the student is left with a longing
an awakening call.
Startled, sometimes scared,
as his ego begins to fade
as her righteousness begins to shatter
as those rules cease to be resourceful
as her beliefs begin to lack power.

The student then opens the heart towards humbleness, and then the master returns and points their eyes towards the mirror of the soul
where enlightenment, teaching, teacher, student have always and will always be one.
There all identity is lost, all sense of self forgotten...the reflection becomes God.

This is the power of the Master.

Message 68
The Star Gate Of The Seven Points[37]
By Brother Djwal

October 6, 2012 - 8:49 AM

Greetings:

The world of the unseen speaks.
Fear not as you begin the remembrance of that which
is blocked by the lack of DNA intelligent wisdom in you,
that can easily be activated by will.

Understand that energy never dies.
Inside of you, you know the way
because inside, the YOU , has never existed:
You have seven known chakras
You have several identities
You have lived a life, that you call life.
Yet you only awaken to it the moment death takes place.

Immortality is not possible without death.
The passage,
the mirror of the unseen of thy own mind.
The moment where all projected apparent realities begins
to unglue itself from the soul.

Death is the ultimate goal of the Master.
Death is the Enlightenment of the Divine.

The transitory is not permanent.
The permanent is static movement.

---

[37] Twelve point Star of David is the shape of the portal where humanity will ascend.

*A paradox life and death are,
yet one and the same.*

*Awakening into reality,
dropping the dream
and creating a new moment.*

*To die is to embrace the now, the love for what is.
Never fear the stage of the Star gate of the Seven Doors or Points,
walk through it choosing the highest light.
Distract not.*

*Teach your children to focus on light,
the day death comes they will be ready.
They will awaken to their own immortal existence
and become enlightened.*

Message 69
By J.K

October 6, 2012 - 12:55 PM

When the inner eye is open, worlds unseen begin to be revealed to the seeker that becomes one with the search as he awakens.

In the new era, the meditator must direct all his force and power towards the one lotus within that will unfold thousands of miracle vibrations towards the universe.

The awareness that every single thought is united with the whole, must remain active until this oneness becomes the obvious and separation becomes a forgotten dream.
As the new era ascends in to its new conscious vibratory frequencies, the one who merges with the all, must remain still and connected to nature.
Easy will it be for the weak mind to pretend to work and be bounded and enslaved by technology.
Before it was time, now the machines you created for good, may have taken power over the human mind.

It is an essential part of enlightenment to prioritize, to remain aware that nature comes first, for that which you prioritize speaks about what you choose to be and create.

Cease as well during meditation all complaints of discomfort, of secret whining of why me, or, why not me?
Cease the low frequency thoughts that create separation, where you see others as lucky, as chosen, and you as a hard worker that never sees its wishes granted.
Rise above the habit of self-limitation through meditation.

Enlightenment belongs to those who are congruent. Simply breathing, and being present, doing what is right.
This is the ultimate power.

Message 70
The Divine Neutrality
By Siddharta

October 8, 2012 - 1:18 PM

ENLIGHTENMENT PER SE does not exist.

It is the grandest illusion in humanity.
It is the one program that detours humanity from truly awakening and getting unplugged from a matrix that feeds itself even from spiritual beliefs.

To be present, untouched by these programs is the true awakening.
To aim for enlightenment is to miss it.
There is no such thing as that. To be enlightened presupposes for many that you are holier than others.

I say unto thee, focus must be moment to moment, being present; this is the true awakening, the ascension of consciousness.
In the times to come, many will awaken and will be unplugged from all the beliefs that bound them to the system of the matrix.

Do meditate.
Do breathe with the awareness of Prana.[38]

Take actions according to the Christiac and Buddha nature
and move forward.

Moment to moment dropping concepts of enlightenment,
dropping beliefs of negative or positive
becoming with this the Divine Neutrality.

I have spoken again.

---

[38] Prana is a Sanskrit word literally meaning 'life-force' the invisible bio-energy or vital energy that keeps the body alive and maintains a state of good health. www.crystalinks.com

Message 71
Kingdom Of Celestial Wisdom
By Serapis Bay

October 10, 2012 - 11:32 AM

The light of prosperity will shine for those that remain unattached to wants.
Distractions abound for the mind unruled
like a dog with his Master.

This must be the commitment of he who commits to a life of awakening.
Master of his mind he must be.

A mind built by character of the highest order.

Distracted not by the Maras[39] that lure the soul into oblivion
Commitment to strength, discipline, morality, flexibility and ease in productivity.
Those who are slaves of the mind shall be lost in the herd of belief systems.
Those who rise beyond thoughts and concepts
To them belongs the kingdom of celestial wisdom.

---

[39] Mara ("bringer of death") demon who harasses the Buddha at the Bodhi Tree. http://orias.berkeley.edu/visuals/buddha

Message 72
Freedom To Be
By Lord Matreya

October 10, 2012 - 10:46 AM

Your need to create stories about reality
must take repose.
Embrace reality as is.

The Master remains present, and accomplishes the task ahead
with passion, commitment and presence.
Never a military approach.
Yet one pointed laser focus.

The true Master understands the language of the intelligent mind
and will only teach that which by experience he has embodied:
Never more, never less.

He lives the path of equanimity...rejoicing at the center of the wheel
of death and life, rising beyond a matrix of pre-conceived reality.

He is free to be....

Message 73
By Lady Nada

October 10, 2012 - 12:11 PM

*Good deeds shall never be seen as hard work or effort,
neither, expect to be paid back.*

*The awakened mind knows this and rejoices in the tranquility of giving:
Mind over power and heart over mind.*

*Actualization of thoughts happens consistently:
A mind at ease,
A body in action,
A spirit in meditation.*

Discipline is an absolute.

Love is the force.

*Propelling the Master to move with the water of soul wisdom;
Ever present,
Ever here,
Ever awake!*

Message 74
Remove Your Hidden Envy
By Sanat Kumara

October 11, 2012 - 10:34 AM

Remove your hidden envy,
your repressed thoughts.

Cease to try to prove unto others how holy you are
and your true holiness shall shine.
Do not proclaim your good deeds out loud,
they have a voice of their own.

Master thy priorities.
Lead time with grace.
Read the sacred scriptures not for accumulation but for practice.
Waste no opportunity to be active.
Procrastination and laziness are the true capital sins.
They blur the siddhi powers that by birthright you possess.

Awaken! Rise!
And the true knowledge of the stars
will descend upon thy psyche.

Remain humble in thy thoughts,
As all shall be revealed.

Message 75
The Return Of The Goddess
By Lady Nada

October 11, 2012 - 10:56 PM

Do not despair for the light of the spit will be radiating tenfold in the times to come
as the unplugging begins to take place.

Massive awakenings will occur.
Hormones of the human form require stabilization as many begin to get free from the moon effect that commands the waters of the subconscious.

The moon has another side,
the side of hidden commands.

Many of them targeted for women to remain high with the tides.
Yet I say unto thee, never in times before a massive female awakening would have taken place.
The pathway of ascension is for the feminine global awakening.
The return of the Mother dressed up as Kali, as Durga.
As Lakshmi,
with the passion of Venus,
the determination of Isis.

The return of the Goddess.
BE ready,
for I Am!

Message 76
To Live Awake One Must Do What Is Right Consistently
By St Germaine

October 12, 2012 - 12:08 AM

To live awake one must do what is right consistently.
To gather with likeminded beings.
To remain loving and focused in the midst of despair.
To radiate generosity of presence and time with thy loved ones.

Live for others and you live the eternal life of spirit.
The Violet Flame is a tool for the willing
The kind,
The leaders,
The lovers.
Truth is the key.
Service the fuel.
Productivity its Power.
It is not for those who wish to sleep.

The flame chooses its target, peels off all identities
and awakens the mind of God within.

I Am the guardian of this Violet Flame
I Am

Message 77
Dropping The Ego
By Kwan Yin

October 12, 2012 - 12:16 AM

Dropping the ego, all sense of "mine"
is not only necessary but a must
if one is to merge with the Ocean of Creation.

Allow no fear based implants to detour you from the use and power if imagery.
Consistently uphold divine thoughts
and serve!

Simple command to sustain what is....

The unveiling has begun.
And it needs a humble mind to receive
the enlightenment of the heart.

Commentary On Part VI
Enlightenment

Knowing others is wisdom, knowing yourself is Enlightenment.
~ Lao Tzu

I used to associate the term *Enlightenment* with the image of a meditating Buddha sitting under a tree in a state of absolute peace and neutrality.

In my research, I discovered that there are many interpretations, teachings and approach of attaining Enlightenment in various cultures. I think these different interpretations are based on own individual and cultural human experiences. Jesus named the Beatitudes, positive and loving statements to enter the Kingdom of Heaven. Moses for example received the Ten Commandments. I perceived the Ten Commandments as laws based of and compliance to an external rule giver instead of self empowering and internally directed. I started to ask myself questions. Is my perception correct? Can it be that in that period this state was necessary to inspire the people to leave Egypt. Or, was the translation of the text accurate?

Whatever the history, the clarity of the messages from the masters changed my perception and I now see Enlightenment as the action oriented state of a conscious person, who is awake, aware of reality and most of all acts upon it. Who is capable of mastering the mind to maintain it to highest vibrations and thus inevitably unplugs from the matrix system.

The synchronicity of what Ivonne and I were focused on continued throughout the entire period of co-creating this book. One day I was walking on the beach with my daughter when suddenly I started talking about the concept of freedom expressed though our thoughts, words and acts. We were diving in the waves of the ocean and I expressed gratefulness for the teachings and life experiences I have been going through to feel free to be as I am. We were celebrating life and putting ourselves with playfulness *In Light* while at the same time Ivonne, sitting in her office, received message number seventy-two.

I realized that these guidelines to turn on the inner light are available for everybody. It only requires the willingness to step up and to come out of the closet.

The messages and transmissions become more intense. Before you continue with Part VII, a short and powerful chapter, I highly suggest to pause, drink some water and visualize the water being a violet color.

PART VII
THE SECRET SOCIETIES

Message 78
By Brother Paul

October 15, 2012 - 4:56 PM

To all those continuing, in secret, the wisdom of the great masters you are called secret societies.

I am here to tell you about the tidings of the new era.
With the new passage of 2012 the ancient scriptures must be unveiled for those in the path of honestly living.
No more can the wisdom of the ancients be put in a jail of control.
Everyone in the path of self-revelation, that has come to know the law of love, is worthy of receiving the commands, the techniques of psycho kinesis and mind mastery.

Imagery is a tool that must be taught to the thousands.
Breathing through the tune of nature must be given to the children

The letters written in the pyramids must be revealed now.
Those secret societies using mind control to enlist souls for your belief systems will begin to collapse.
The one society is the universe.
The one religion is the law of truth.
The one program that works is the one of love.

Anything not coming from this essence will cease to exist.
The time has come.

Message 79
By Mary

October 15, 2012 - 4:57 PM

*Rosicrucians[40] hear this well,
the chalice of the feminine must be unveiled.*

*The time for the Magdalene spirit has come to be unleashed in humanity.
Join forces with the ones that allow the spirit of the goddess to permeate the minds of men.*

*Nobility, stability, and grace are the characteristics of the true initiated ones.
Awaken now in all your members the timely call for liberation.*

---

[40] A secret worldwide brotherhood claiming to possess esoteric wisdom handed down from ancient times. The name derives from the order's symbol, a combination of a rose and a cross. Its origins are obscure. Its earliest known document, *Account of the Brotherhood* (1614), tells the story of the supposed founder, Christian Rosenkreuz ("Rose Cross"), allegedly born in 1378, who is said to have acquired his wisdom on trips to the Middle East and imparted it to his followers on his return to Germany. www.merriam-webster.com

Message 80
By Father Hu-Nab, Kum

October 15, 2012 - 5:03 PM

Vatican; Oh you fools, haven't you created much sorrow already?
The pure Beings harmed by the apparent beatitude of your robes, are souls that are emissaries from the laws of the council.
They sacrificed themselves in order to test the honesty of your movement.

Thou shall be no more, the power you emanate comes from fear and control.
These obsolete programs will not give you more power.

The people you lead will begin massive awakening.
The souls will remember who they are.

The Christ will speak to them in the church of their own hearts,
not through the facility that condemns humanity as sinners.

A new church must be edified
a council of enlightenment
where the leaders are those who can guide humanity to master their human needs.

A council of true lovers of life of those who hold life as sacred.
A council that will be chosen by the masters of dimensions 11, 12, 15 and the Universe AH.
They have already been chosen.
No prosecution or lies bestowed upon them will eradicate their power.

They have been chosen.
They have been blessed.
They have been initiated already
in the pyramids where the Itzaes were born once.
They will all gather and they have gathered
in the center of the land of the many.

*Their leaders will awaken too.
They are called entrepreneurs,
Mothers, Teachers, motivators.*

*To them belongs the power of the Council of Earth that will be in charge to teach wisdom to the ignorant.
To create the new school of thought.
To teach the new ways where the DNA will create new realities
and to bring the mastery of living to the simple basic teaching of loving and being present here and now.*

Message 81
By M.Krishna

October 15, 2012 - 5:06 PM

Oh races of beings that control Earth.
Oh reptiles, Neburians, and the races that interfered long ago,
Thy contract is over.
We are coming back.
There is no disease you can create.
No thought you can radiate.
No illusion you can manifest that will distract
the coming back of the light of truth.

Remember your agreement.
And if thou forget,
we are here to make sure the new agreements take place.
Leaders, puppets, and the holders of the earth's moneys,
the time has arrived to go through bio-regenesis

The true leader is silent.
The true blessing is already given.

Anger, envy, greed, jealousy are the true capital sins.
Kindness, generosity, and truth are the power liberators.
They have been unleashed.

Humanity will ascend.

Commentary On Part VII
Secret Societies

The very word "secrecy" is repugnant in a free and open society; and we are as a people inherently and historically opposed to secret societies, to secret oaths, and to secret proceedings. ~ John F. Kennedy

This section is short, the messages powerful: inviting us to look at how humanity has been captured and controlled on all levels of our society.

Fear-based rules created and spread by official institutions exercise massive control. The Vatican is named here and I think we will hear more in future about this institution. Power battles on and beyond earth between human and not human races, lies, corruption, violence, viruses and conspiracies. The list is long. For weeks I researched so many different sources of information that at one time I realized the saying *less is more* and to use my own intuition of interpreting certain events.

I came to the conclusion that what really matters, is to focus on raising my consciousness, support others with this process and to ascend. In short: keep moving forward!

The messages reveal that important knowledge has been hidden for ages and kept in the hands of few groups some with the intent to maintain power, and some with the intent to protect the ancient wisdom. In one of the messages the Rosicrucian Society is even called directly to reveal information. Once again the messages here are open and clear. It is time to step out of the secret realms and reveal truth.

With an increasing curiosity I continued reading as the Masters kept on surprising me with their revelations and the appearance of new or unexpected masters who shared their messages.

I invite you now to leave the world of secret plots and to enter into the world of the angels.

PART VIII
THE ASCENDED ANGELS SPEAK

Message 82
Prepare To Heal
By Gabriel

October 16, 2012 - 9:52 PM

When the light of truth begins to descend upon the ignorant thoughts of men the radiating awakening will take place.

Male/female children, sentient beings in unison dancing and celebrating the good tidings of regeneration and birth of the new wisdom.

This is the moment where the healing of all dis-eases will begin to take place. The creation of a man made ailment called Aids, will disappear, as man begins to let go of the herd mentality that keeps this thought process in place.

The creation of fake inputs in to the immune system of humanity, called viruses, will no longer be able to kill, deteriorate or damage the human form as the hertz frequency generator of the mind turns on itself to generate the appropriate sound healing that will protect itself from the harms of the automatic pilot matrix.
So fear no more and never more. As the time of ultimate healing approaches, where the truth shall lead: as the man follows the planet, and the planet follows the rhythm of the universe.

This celestial cosmos follows the ultimate truth, and truth itself will descend as I have spoken upon the face of Earth, and all the cosmological communities of the higher spirit.

Prepare to Heal,

I have arrived, I am the healer, I am healing, I am.

Message 83
Angelic Cosmic Evolution
By Michael

October 16, 2012 - 9:59 PM

From angelic we have ascended our wings now to the ether and the portal of the Rishi world, waiting for access.
Those of us, who generated the tidings of good karma, have begun the process of angelic cosmic evolution.

We cannot stay the same as thou all may notice in thyself.
To make you believe we are and have been the same for eons is to support a system of comfortability, where religions, winged beings
and outside power, seem to exist and be more powerful than thou.

This is not so, as it is far away from the truth.
We have aligned with thee all, evolved.
So it is that we have been granted the next step of our evolution and thus remain guardians and alert to thy own evolutionary stages.

With my sword, let us all cut the cords towards the matrix that binds us to the lure of hidden pleasures and apparent dark forces.

I shall use this sword of truth to cut the ailments of cancer, leukemia, and the projected phenomena of lethal weapons shared by pesticides, and polluted foods.

Time is of the essence,
and I remain a loyal servant and guardian of humanity.

Message 84
By Rafael

October 16, 2012 - 10:06 PM

*Healers, healing and healed
all one and the same.
Autism,
anxiety,
mental disorders,
come to my arms as I bathe them in blue healing powers.*

*The evolution that is taking place has granted me more of that which I serve.
To receive the initiation of healer,
thou must be in command of thy mind
thy ethical wings must be the fuel for the healing thou offer.*

*Humanity lost has created the ailments that here and now I have mentioned.
The children struck by these human projections will begin spontaneous healing.
Blame is a disease that must be eradicated from earth.*

*Invoke me and I shall serve thee as reminder
with blue light of the spirit.*

We are now allowed to heal instantaneously, those who believe in their own power.

Commentary On Part VIII
The Ascended Angels Speak

If instead of a gem, or even a flower, we should cast the gift of a loving thought into the heart of a friend, that would be giving as the angels give.
~ George MacDonald

Ivonne and I were both not expecting receiving messages coming from the realm of the Angels.

There are different interpretations of the role and identity of angels, depending one's cultural and/or religious education. In general they are named the messengers of God, or divine helpers.

In this book there are only three of them sharing messages. They are Archangels.[41] They desire to let us know that also in their realm many of them experienced an evolutionary process similar to humanity and that many of them are guardians of humanity and offer their support when we call upon them.

The message of Rafael states clearly the use of the blue as a healing power. This reminds me to call upon this power and to visualize the color with remembered awareness together with the Codes of AH or Bach Flower remedies or when doing energetic bodywork.

In addition, they lovingly remind us of our own healing power!

The transmissions of the Angels were for me a humble reminder that there are many sentient beings watching and supporting the Earth and humanity right now.

More wisdom is waiting to be revealed in the next chapter, Part IX where more masters showed up with subtle though powerful transmissions.

---

[41] 1: a chief angel. 2 *plural* : an order of angels. Middle English, from Anglo-French or Late Latin; Anglo-French *archangle*, from Late Latin *archangelus*, from Greek *archangelos*, from *archi-* + *angelos* angel First Known Use: 12th century. www.merriam-webster.com

PART IX
WISDOM FROM THE BEYOND

Message 85
By Kwan Yin

October 17, 2012 - 11:24 PM

*Never judge any stage, school, church, or religion in humanity.
To judge or even speak poorly about anything is to invite the same condemnation to your own energy field.*

*Understand everything as a passing breeze, as an evolutionary stage.
Each being will be held in the right teaching environment until the lesson is learned and they move on to the next evolutionary step.*

*The soul is already at home during this process.
The one experiences itself as a sentient being and learns about himself in the school of experience.*

Thus, focus at all times in whatever stage and doctrine thou may choose to be, in ceasing all judgment, this will take you closer to the portal of self-realization where you enter the cosmic school of thought field generation.

Remember to breathe with awareness, and understand that truth is beyond understanding. Its invisibility can only be learned by the vibration of presence.

*For that which is spoken and seen this is no longer the truth.
Understand this and embrace the essential.*

Message 86
By Rah-Mah-El

October 17, 2012 - 11:30 PM

To bring the soul to harmonic vibration
the medicine for dis-alignments will be given in liquid nectars and
sacred geometrical forms.
Sound, water, shape, and color, these are the new vibratory remedies for re-establishing soul-psyche connection.

The portal of 2012 allows for the transmutation of thought to take place in the higher dimensions where the Rishi masters live.

Pyramids of vibration are to be built inside the mind of man; thought process must be aimed towards creating a ratio of higher frequencies that builds the trinity aspect of creation with every word, action and thought chosen to be created.

Start with learning the skills of sacred alchemy,
the time for humanity to receive this lesson has finally come.

Those who are ready will be contacted.
Humility is the key to enter this new knowledge.

Message 87
By Ah-Mon-Rha

October 17, 2012 - 11:35 PM

The structure of thought looks like this:
Pick up a grain of sand from the dessert.
Blow the exhaling breath of life on to it.
Watch it disappear in front of your eyes.

Yet, the grain has merged with the floor, or with the flower,
or with the water, and travels and becomes one
with anything it touches.

Small particle it is, yet it impacts the whole.
It builds phenomena, it generates nature.
It vibrates recorded DNA history of creation.

Never disregard the power of a single thought.
The mustard seed, as the grain of sand,
is the master power of creation.

Message 88
By Isis

October 17, 2012 - 11:43 PM

*The creation of beauty
is a shrine in the heavens.*

*Oh the mortal thought becomes immortal in its embrace.
I am the transcendent aspect of soul beautification.*

*With me all men can reach the heightened state of
devotional embrace with its creator.*

*I reside in every being and every being emanates from me.
I am Isis, I am Sophia, I am the one goddess in the heart of creation.*

*Return through the coiled awakening path.
Unleash the energy of sensuality,
reverence, grace and humility.*

*The entrance points towards the gifts of my wisdom
that, when properly observed,
birth the new soul fire beings that many call the awakened ones.
Transcending with this thought;
As there is a realm that creates without thought process.
Intent is born before thought,
such is the beauty of I AM.*

Message 89
By The Nameless

October 17, 2012 - 11:51 PM

Cosmology will show you the essence of what seems real.
It will teach you the skills of building planes, star gates and portals in the sky that you call the heavens.
You will learn how to be a master architect of creation.

The school of humanity is a station
where those who awaken can move forward to other realms and dimensions.

Entering the invisibility schools of
1. Thoughts
2. Intent
3. Mastery of the elements
4. Embodiment of soul unity
5. Vibratory universal equanimity.
Once the stages are complete
the soul meets again with itself as the one creator.
Choosing either to create a new mathematical algorithm or to create its own universe.
where it will create its´ own races
Its´ own founders
Its´ own beings.
Thus experience itself as the creator in the all and everything.
This is the cycle where we learn to become Gods.

Commentary On Part IX
Wisdom From The Beyond

The beautiful souls are they that are universal, open,
and ready for all things.
~ Michel de Montaigne

The more I went through the messages the more I realized how great it is to experience life here on earth during this period of important planetary and human shift. Imagine the privilege we all have to witness the revelation of truth which has been hidden for eons.

This awareness supported an expansion of my heart to see more and more of the overall meaning of life as an individuated soul on one hand and connected with the collective at the other hand.

I highly appreciated message number eighty-eight as given by Isis. For me this message represented the awakening of the feminine energy that has been a wave moving across the planet; to remember the necessity to awaken powerful creative and magnetic energy of the women and also the feminine energy that flows in the men. An energy which transmutes the violence of words with sensuality, grace and elegance.

This Part IX was a gentle reminder for me of the individual power of choosing. With our choice we create our own reality by breathing our way through the space of Universal beauty called life, and balancing the masculine and feminine energy.

I experienced this chapter as a gentle entrance and preparation for the next chapter, Part X.
And I am pleased to invite you to meet the members of the Council of AH, coming from a universe beyond this 15 dimensional time matrix system. The transmissions given by their messages are even more intensified than before.

PART X
THE COUNCIL OF AH

Message 90
By Equileh Ah Rah Meh
Honorary Guardian Observant of The Laws of AH

October 18, 2012 - 8:53 PM

If thy actions injure another's life:
If thy suggestions bring others to drop the values of spirit to enjoy the mundane, the temporal they shall not receive the fruit of karma but thou will.
It is not a threat.
It is a loving warning so you make the right decisions when thou give thy opinion.

Thy children will no longer, with this 2012 passage, hold the unpaid and uncompleted situations that thy field didn't want to carry.
For eons this was the way of the law.
The children will pay the debts of their fathers,
so the fathers can learn the lesson.
Such sacrifice is no longer needed.
The new children, new beings are coming to Earth not to heal the parents;
But to adjust planetary alignment,
to raise human consciousness,
to activate galactic awareness,
to initiate the new journey towards humanity becoming universal member of the council of the Absolute Harmonic Universe.

Such is now that thy responsibility begins to take back the reflected projections thou have done unto others.
Complete thy loose ends,
heal and amend the cycles that require it.
Move forward!
Ethics and values will no longer be a prophet's dream, or a philosopher's writings.
They will be as necessary as blood is to the body and oxygen to the breath of life.
Carry them with you and thou shall ascend.
Drop them, and mortal thou remain.

Message 91
By Sath, Kam
AH First Officer of the Council of AH

October 18, 2012 - 8:46 PM

Tested will be the soaring spirit that can transmute
the dense in to the subtle,
the dark in to the luminous,
the impossible in to the done.

Thou all shall see beyond the disruptions.
Cross the wall through the power of invisibility.
Go beyond the mundane, the habits,
the ignorance reflected by others in thee as thee walk
the path of transformational mind transmutation.

Create a field of protection around you
with the great truth
any injury
caused to thee by another will bounce immediately back to its source.

As well, make sure to remain impeccable.
As now the gateways of instant results of the laws has re-opened
and thou must treat one another as thou desire to be treated.

Belong to the light.
Make the right choices.

Message 92
By Gah-Ehl-Rah
Master Emissary of Mind-physics of AH

October 18, 2012 – 8:58 PM

*When Earth ascends thou shall all be welcomed
in to the new dimension of thought where mind will
begin to awaken its full potentiality.*

*Mind is a tool that is contained in all of the universes.
We all use the same tool for manifestation.
The capacity and ways to use it differently based on the evolution of the heart
and soul of each individuated particle of source called beings.*

*In the Council we summon the gentle souls,
the kindred hearts
the benevolent ethical beings that will, with honor,
carry the next assignments eagerly in to the universal collective mind.*

*Thus we ascend together towards the remembrance of the oneness,
for the joy of the generation of more of the experience of what is.
Understand not these words with the brain.
Use the mind intelligence that resides in the heart.*

*Mind is not contained in the head.
It is boundless of forms.
It thinks beyond itself.
It creates this very moment.*

Message 93
By Ha-Ehl-Yeh
AH Guardian of Universal Emissaries
of Light Council of AH

October 18, 2012 - 9:41 PM

Do not waste a second of the program of Time.

Thou shall have learned by now the importance of the skill of its management.
Do not take for granted quiet hours of meditation as well,
neither the importance of working with eagerness when the sun rises in the house of spirit.

These, what seem daily basic human endeavors are necessary training pieces for the next evolutionary stage we begin on December 23rd on Earth.

A new cycle of 2528 years shall begin. Being that in 2538 we will revisit the new advancement and what worked and what didn't and decide upon the creation of New Earth programs or not.

Do not detour thy focus by any interferences or manipulative strategies that uses the matrix to distract the path of the light deliverers.
Continue no matter what.
The priorities shall be spoken loudly when the time comes.
Drop the explanations, others will not understand the great integrity program, as it can not be spoken.

The devotion and commitment towards contribution must be the marriage of the deliverers of the way of the invisible teachings
that now descend upon earth in the timely stages of mind conscious evolution.

Message 94
By Eh-Nah-Yah-El
Quantum Scholar Council of AH

October 18, 2012 - 9:58 PM

The Fibonacci numbers[42] are sequences of control from the matrix that projects the aleatory[43] waves of its manifestation.

You can create your own sequence by sound/tone/color.
Choose the hertz that suit you best, choose the color that attracts the most.
Choose the fragrance, the essential, the right code.

Mix it all together and thou create a sequence where the necessary
veil lifter appears in the psyche and the soul at the same time.
Bridging soul/mind with the universal intelligence.
Rekindling the remembrance of its power thus as a creator.
Attaining form as a sun,
the body of the stars,
and the force of the light speed beyond time.

---

[42] Origin of Fibonacci: Leonardo *Fibonacci* died*ab*1250 Italian mathematician. First Known Use: 1914. In mathematics, the Fibonacci numbers are an integer in the infinite sequence 1, 1, 2, 3, 5, 8, 13, … of which the first two terms are 1 and 1 and each succeeding term is the sum of the two immediately preceding. www.merriam-webster.com

[43] By chance or luck, uncertain outcome. Free online Dictionary.

Message 95
By Kah-Mah-Ehl
Wisdom Elder Council of AH

October 19, 2012 - 4:03 PM

The powers of the minds will open up.
Sooner or later the matrix will not be able to hook and plug the minds of men
by the use of their own weakness, ignorance and non inquired thoughts.

Soon enough the effects of the drugs, artificial colorants and preservatives that
were created by the such called Illuminati, will no longer be able to manipulate
the system of the human body.

These beings that based their reign with fear, are but puppets of the races that
control them inside the matrix.
They created all these ailments, all these artificial weapons to control the mind
of the masses.
For it is well known by the governments and the higher intelligences in them
that the mind of man is the ultimate creator.
They try to keep dormant this consciousness as these will remove their power
when awakening takes place.

They were told the awakening of the mind will begin its process on December 23rd.
It will actually have begun before that.
Knowing this they will create what are called third and fourth wars.
New threats and new fear strategies
to keep humanity living within herd mentality.

Yet, the new children,
the avatars incarnated will awaken
and the diseases created by man
will vanish.

The more the man masters his thoughts,
the more peace will behold Earth and its sentient beings.

Message 96
By Ah-Mhan-Tat
Great Father Founder Council of AH

October 20, 2012 - 10:45 AM

At the point where higher assignments will be given for those who desire to ask, the sacred information will be given to them.

Yet a higher contract is signed immediately upon receiving it.
Anything that is out of alignment with the assignment will be revealed for the individual to work on himself.
Not on the others.

It is an illusion and a dishonor to the universal laws to try to change, and project your own teachings, limitations, and projections and generated belief statements unto others.

The true master sustains a congruent action/thought/word/mind set all of the time and beyond it.
Rise and see.

We will speak to many,
few will take action.
Even less than few will remain congruent
in the probable futures that exist.

There will be success in few.
All are meant to succeed if the heart and mind is aligned with congruency.

We begin now.

Message 97
By Babaji Nagaraj
Ascended Master Representative Guest at the Council of AH

October 20, 2012 - 10:49 AM

Everything is energy.
The creation of duality is made by those who teach others about it.
Who tell others of their wrongs.
Who create fixed scenarios in an environment of inflexibility and self-righteousness.

The Man that cannot see beyond this, will remain in a cycle where success will not be attainable.
It will be as it has always been,
a great star
a great hope
then loss of values
and wondering why and where to go?

Endless stories of civilizations.
awaken to kindness, equanimity and understanding.
See all as appropriate.
Humble thyself
and then rise.

Message 98
By Lha-Tzah-Eh
Honorary Member, Council of AH

October 20, 2012 - 10:52 AM

Everything, all observation of reality is a mere projection of it.
The beings in Planet Earth assigned to support others awakening,
must go through a fast of humility.

The children must be treated with respect at all times.
The master that is annoyed
and looses patience when in their presence is no master.

The master must not label anything as wrong,
this contains blame and judgment,
the greatest vices that are to be eradicated from the universe for it to ascend.

No one, can enter AH with these traits:
Prejudice,
Righteousness,
Blame and judgment.
Believing YOU KNOW IT ALL
is a sure ticket for stagnation.

Surrender it all,
resist nothing.

We have spoken.

Be one with the great integrity.

Message 99
By Hay Merth Hau Hu
Honorary Guardian of the Law of Cause and Effect, Member of the Council of AH

October 20, 2012 - 11:23 AM

The great beings of AH that were planted on Earth to guide the Hu Masters that have lost the path before by greed.
Now they are retaking their missions to support humanity to ascend.
These great beings will not be able to stay long in the fields of Earth mechanics when the energy surrounding them is of control,
procrastination,
and need for sleep.

The Beings of AH were sent to model productivity, time mastery, mastery of the field that creates thoughts, words and to remind all to live in the present moment.

AH beings exist by the energy of congruency,
especially those who have mastered humbleness.

The ones that say they are from AH yet are still in a human learning process, can be spotted as they think they know it all.

Humility again is the new ascended Rishi structure program.
Those who surrender to this energy shall become the nothingness
the selfless,
the invisible force
that generates good and benevolence for the sake of divine love.

Message 100
By Mataji
Guest Honorary Earth mechanics Consultant for the Council of AH

October 20, 2012 - 11:28 AM

One by one the veils of illusion will fall
as the Divine Mother begins her dance towards taking back her children with her
to the source field realm beyond the matrixes.
That by now are projected in 15,000 different collective universes.
The mind of God shall expand.
Such will her womb,
in the arms of experience she will carry the ones that are to move to the next universe to bring the tidings of AH.

Many shall depart from Earth
sooner than a mind would desire
the mortal one.

Yet, for the sake of the creator existence and the reaching of the tipping point of universal harmony and the reign of peace,
these beings are to change form.
To travel in the Merkabahs of Ascension
with the support of the sacred codes
that will take them to simultaneously travel, teach and support the civilizations that are already calling and waiting for them.

The time has come.
The higher consciousness migration of the AH species has begun.

Message 101
By Yeshua Ha Yuh
Guardian Omni Love Field Frequencies
Counselor for The Council of AH

October 20, 2012 - 12:08 PM

The man who treats the feminine with any disregard for her vulnerable power will encounter the programs of self-revelation necessary to re-educate himself towards the importance of his own feminine energy evolving
in the awakening of the female era.

Amends are to be taken place by honoring and respecting the polarities created by the mind that unruled by will has randomly participated in the MATRIX PROGRAMS.

Listen well.
The ascension process is very simple
and the unplugging from the un-natural shields is possible.
Breathe,
Meditate,
do what is right.

We will take care of the rest.

Commentary On Part X
The Council of AH

*We all come from our own little planets. That's why we're all different.
That's what makes life interesting.*
~ Robert E. Sherwood

Great was my surprise to see messages directly coming from members of the Council of AH with their names and titles.

I noticed how The factor "time" shows up through the entire book. The Council of AH also reiterates the importance of mastering time. Personally, I experienced challenges in the "use of time." Somehow I managed to manifest these by creating states of overwhelm by thinking the belief that I had not enough time available to do all I wished to do. Ivonne, who has become a master in time management showed me one day a wonderful way of scheduling the different tasks I wish to accomplish. At night message 93 arrived starting with: " Do not waste a second of the program of Time".

Since I have begun to use this time management schedule, I experience even more productivity and joy doing the tasks. Moreover, I notice that time adapts itself to my schedule instead of the contrary.

While the messages of the Council of AH were being received, my body again entered a cleansing and integration process. I created space for self care as I am aware that this is all part of the unplugging procedure!

As I integrated the previous messages, I experienced an expansion of my mind and spirit beyond this home, called Earth. I was gifted with a glimpse into other universes, the support we receive and the knowledge that there was yet more to come.

Indeed, more gifts came.
And with this in mind I invite you to enter the last parts of *Unplug Your Mind*!

PART XI

SCIENTISTS OF UNIVERSAL CREATION

Message 102
By Hunab Kah Hul
Quantum Chief Soul Creator
Medical Universal Scientist
Guest Honor for the Council of AH

October 20, 2012 - 11:01 PM

The microscopic scales of the phenomena[44] on Earth and the inner realm of each individuated source conscious particle will begin to collapse. As each thought now will generate exact dual and wave like behaviors between all universes of matter and energy.
These phenomena will unleash the siddhi powers of the mind. Since the energies are increasing, the extremes of all stressors and manifestations will bring forward the emergence of collective awakening for universal ascension.

The beings of ten thousand universes have begun the process to support the Earth to ascend as part of their own manifestation. All thought particles are being focused on Earth, and the dynamic of this impact will generate an evident transcendence of form, matter and spirit so Earth can go in to the next evolutionary stage.

We all will be absorbed by the mind of the divine, awakening with this the ONE awareness, within our soul memory. We must but vibrate the energies of procreation, and set our divine intention to the highest of aim. With this all, polarity of negativity is impossible to be vibrated as creativity takes over.
Allow ecstasy to unfold from the heart center to bathe the particles with this energy motion.
It creates ecstasy. This ecstasy is the prerequisite.

The quantum essence of all acts will also be shifting the portal of sexuality, in which procreation of beings takes place. It must be sublimated at this stage,

---

[44] Any state or process known through the senses rather than by intuition or reasoning; any fact, circumstance, or experience that is apparent to the sensed and that can be scientifically described or appraised.

as this will be the drive to create the next powerful existence. Eventually this portal will transcend by union with intent solely. Until then, evolve thy sexual ways, as the quantum mechanics of the creator shift, and the wave and dual like vibrations merge to generate the state of awakened consciousness in the center of the heart of the one.

Message 103
By Hel-Tha-Hu
Universal Architect Engineer,
Member of the Council of AH

October 20, 2012 - 11:11 PM

New planets shall be created and the hidden ones will be unveiled.
The governments of Earth have secret information regarding the way the astral and the planetarium forces work.

Regardless of the findings the frequencies generated by feldspars[45], metals, magnesium, aluminum, helium, hydrogen, water & gas will unite and create a collapsing bomb that will shift atmospheres of psyche and physical activities.

All the dark bodies, and all the families of stars will radiate and pulsate even more light than before.
A new sun shall be discovered.

While this takes place the process for New Earth generation will begin, where all the sentient beings that vibrate desire for life will be selected to ascend and awaken as the great masters have done so.

This will create minds that awaken and stay present in the now, which generates a nuclear field that shifts the realities of darkness in to a massive awakening of light.
The structures are set in place.
The thoughts that align with the new vibrations have begun to arrive.
We are ready; to create the new Earth and the system called the Ahmrai Galaxy.

---

[45] Feldspar is by far the most abundant group of minerals in the earth's crust, forming about 60% of terrestrial rocks. Most deposits offer sodium feldspar as well as potassium feldspar and mixed feldspars. Feldspars are primarily used in industrial applications for their alumina and alkali content. The term feldspar encompasses a whole range of materials. Most of the products we use on a daily basis are made with feldspar: glass for drinking, glass for protection, fiberglass for insulation, the floor tiles and shower basins in our bathrooms, and the tableware from which we eat. www.ima-na.org

Message 104
By G-HAY-El-HI
Physics Tao Guardian, Council of AH

October 20, 2012 - 11:22 PM

The orbits of the mind and heart will begin to move accordingly to non-linear forces. What will happen when all Humans are focusing on ascension?
This will generate a dance between the forward motion of their thoughts contained in the intelligent space and the pull of the sacred gravity[46] that propels the forward movement for humanity.

Evolution will take place.

While the pull towards fear is stronger than ever, the power of presence and consciousness humans have manifested will end the tug-of-war between the forces that go forth and against the human collective awakening.

To create the necessary speed of awakening, the masters must:

1. *Create momentum[47] and bring their students forward as they focus strongly on the mastery of thought and mind.*
2. *Command with intent, the gravity to attract these mastery of thoughts and bring it to the Universe of Absolute Harmony*

---

[46] (1)the gravitational attraction of the mass of the earth, the moon, or a planet for bodies at or near its surface. (2) : a fundamental physical force that is responsible for interactions which occur because of mass between particles, between aggregations of matter (as stars and planets), and between particles (as photons) and aggregations of matter, that is 10^{-39} times the strength of the strong force, and that extends over infinite distances but is dominant over macroscopic distances especially between aggregations of matter —called also *gravitation, gravitational force*. www.merriam-webster.com

[47] 1: a property of a moving body that the body has by virtue of its mass and motion and that is equal to the product of the body's mass and velocity; *broadly* : a property of a moving body that determines the length of time required to bring it to rest when under the action of a constant force or moment. 2 : strength or force gained by motion or by a series of events. www.merriam-webster.com

3. *As the pull and forces between momentum and gravity take place, all inferences must be dispelled by continuous good deeds and proper meditations*
4. *While gravity pulls thoughts into AH, the forces will attain balance when mind is focused on the now.*
5. *Keep moving forward so that speed attains more momentum than the gravity pull, which would bring the intent to collapse, when focus is lost.*

Simple Steps:

Thou shall remember; the forces of the non-doing and doing will be the father and mother of the birth of balance.

Commentary On Part XI
Scientists Of Universal Creation

First comes thought; then organization of that thought, into ideas and plans; then transformation of those plans into reality. The beginning, as you will observe, is in your imagination. ~ Napoleon Hill

Here we are gifted with highest scientific teachings of evolution and description and impact of collective thought: The realization that the thoughts of ten thousand universes are literally uplifting and supporting the Earth and her inhabitants increases my state of gratitude and humbleness.

The messages are so powerful that I had to read and reread them. This process was followed by long moments of silence. Over four days I observed out of body experiences, and shifts taking place within my body mainly in the head area. I reminded myself to take care of both the physical and mental body. I drank more water and added more (green) vegetables to my daily menu.

The power of thought and the simple instructions to awaken are described in a way that any being, willing to unplug from this matrix system, can apply.
I realize that whatever I experience as a reality, I remain focused on the present moment and treat myself and others with kindness and highest respect.

This is the way I think anyone can evolve and ascend in awareness.

We arrive at Part XII, where final instructions are revealed and blessings are given from the highest realms.

It is time to receive!

PART XII

FINAL INSTRUCTIONS FOR THE SONS & DAUGHTERS OF EARTH

Message 105
By The Father Tah-Tah,
Great Founder Father of AH

October 21, 2012 - 12:12 AM

Dear Sons and Daughters;
The time has come for thee to come back to me,
as a Mother & Father as I AM the ONE.
I contain my soul in thee, and this is my benevolent advice so you can remember who you are, and the you as me; I AM.

1. *Bring thy mind under control through gradual steps and systematic discipline.*
2. *Strengthen thy will; perseverance of drill is a must as you come back to the awareness of absolute oneness.*
3. *When meditating, allow the thoughts to move, run, walk, and be free. Watch them with detachment, observe their activity, study them, what do they do? How do they move? How do they think? What?*
4. *Watch them, to tame them thou must observe them, love them and set them free...awaken the observant consciousness.*
5. *Thou must love each and one and all of thy thoughts. One thought judged, and seen as negative will come back to teach thee about truth. Love it all, and with this end all violence. Realize that judgment and blame are the distractors for thy path of self-realization, and each thought against another is self-violence exponential.*
6. *Let go of ego desires, vain speech; select wisely thy studies, readings, and surroundings.*
7. *Gather with love and become this love. Give up on fighting, proving, defending and righteousness; the treasure that awaits for you when you resist nothing is this:*
   I AM

Message 106
By The Mother OMAH
Great ONE Mother of AH

October 21, 2012 – 12:24 AM

Beloved Child, sentient being of my womb, as a Great Mother I come.
Follow my instructions and prepare thy body for the active ascension, imagining thy body and mind are strong; I gave thee imagination as a medicine, not as an ailment.

Start using it with power.
Start with thy body, as it will support you to cross the ocean of ascension and life.
Release all false sense-hood of weakness, as the strong will be the ones to cross the waters of the Bardo[48].
Activate self-faith and unbounded love. This will fuel your scalar waves in to more momentum.

Focus on this imagery morning and evening, focusing on manifesting a state of calmness, this will give thy body and mind the proper training to remain serene in the midst of the chaos projected right now. As thou inner sun goes through the portal of transcendence and ends cycles in the Bardo of transmutation.

Wish for all sentient beings happiness, at all times, this creates a surrounding field of absolute protection for thee.
Invoke to receive knowledge and wisdom, and apply it child…apply it…
Remove all dyspepsia[49], embrace and become one with the ocean of bliss, and propagate the news. Apathetic minds are the biggest contagion for others,

---

[48] The term bardo is a general term which literally means "in-between" and in this context denotes a transitional state, or what Victor Turner calls a *liminal* situation. The bardo concept is an umbrella term which includes the transitional states of birth, death, dream, transmigration or afterlife, meditation, and spiritual luminosity. For the dying individual, the bardo is the period of the afterlife that lies in between two different incarnations. www.spiritualtravel.org

[49] 1: indigestion. 2: ill humor (disgruntlement). www.merriam-webster.com

rise as the ultimate medical healer, the one that uses joy for restoration of soul blossoming.

Heal with this all ailments, all diseases, and start with this, living as God Creator. Bless thee my child.

Message 107
By Tah-Tah-Yeh
Great Grandfather Founder of Gaia

October 21, 2012 - 12:45 AM

At this point children thou must drag thy minds and heal its non-stability.
Fix it in the glory of God that resides within.
Time is of the essence.

Aim for the highest state of being. This will collapse the programs of the Matrix and create a slow down script where you can exit it and create your own to ascend in to alignment with the one mind.

Purify, transcend, and meditate. Purify, transcend, release, and reflect, as the purer the mind, the easier it is to attain mastery.
Purity of the mind must be insisted upon and activate higher morality. Release the deeper impressions of limitations. Reach with this the gateways of supra-consciousness that are opening thanks to the star gates on planet Earth, once again, in the thirteen-year cycle that approaches closing.
Release the Maras, the demons, the distractions created not by outside forces but by your own mind.

MASTER THE MIND.

Message 108
By Eah-Rtha
Gestalt Founder Mothers & Fathers of Earth

October 21, 2012 - 1:01 AM

Beloved Beings,

A gestalt I AM. For thousands of eons of times, I have watched your growth, your choices, and your transcendent moments.
I know each and one of thy aspirations and dreams.

I have fed thee, and hosted you as I remained open and watching thy life stages. Now I come let thee know this:
Distract not with Fireballs, Meteors, Signs and storms falling in to specific mathematical algorithmic spaces.
Stay close to the pyramids of the soul, stay away from places where fire and wind are talking as lessons to the necessary beings.

The moment of alchemy has arrived.
The test thou shall pass. The comet will announce my presence.
We have returned.
With thy mind you will and must change and create a new world.

In 2025 I shall return to speak.

I AM Here, I am Earth and I AM.

Humanity will survive.
If Reconnection with Earth takes place, it will, it has, it is done.

Commentary On Part XII
Final Instructions For The Sons & Daughters Of Earth

I've read the last page of the Bible. It's all going to turn out all right.
~ Billy Graham

What more can I say than expressing my deepest gratitude for these final blessings after having journeyed a sacred and powerful initiation;

The gift from the Father Founder of AH transmitting us a complete protocol how to master the mind.

The gift from the Mother Great One, Mother of AH on how to use the imagination to strengthen our body and mind.

The gift from the Great Grandfather Founder of Gaia on the importance of purifying the mind.

The gift of the Gestalt Founder Mothers and Fathers of Earth confirming their presence, nurturing and protection.

May your journey of unplugging unfold into highest awakened presence.

It is done.

Thank you and with Love,

Sylvia Dokter

VISUALIZATION
TO BE USED WITH THE MATRIX UNPLUG STAGE I CODE OF AH©

Code of AH ©Ivonne Delaflor Alexander

This first code of the *Matrix Unplug 12 Codes of AH Program* works very well with Part I of this book. The use of the code will support you as you integrate the transmissions and initiations received through the messages.

Visualization

Focus on the center of the code.

Take 3 deep inhales through the nose
and slowly exhale 3 times through the mouth.

Inhale the code through your third eye (the spot between your eyebrows). With the next exhale send the code down through your body, through your feet to the center of earth.

On the next inhale bring the code up and visualize it about 3,5 Feet above your head. Then with the next exhale send the code down to your first chakra, which is located at the base of the spine in the tailbone area.

Breathe slowly, relax.

Now say out loud or mentally the following intent:

It is commanded in the name of Divine Love and by the laws of the Golden Liquid Realms that the Matrix Unplug Stage I Code of AH infuses my chakras and brain centers, on all levels of my awareness. To awaken my true self and to clear and let go of all matrix system programmed misperceptions and limitations which do not resonate with the highest frequencies of this code. Transmute and transform these into clear choices, absolute presence and full restoration of the adrenal glands to its original divine function. For my highest good and in line with my Higher Self, Now!
I am Freedom, I am Clarity, I am Gratitude.
As it is stated so it is done.
Thank You.

While the highest frequencies of this code calibrate your energetic field, proceed to direct the code 12 times from the crown chakra (on top of the head) to the feet.
When you exhale the code goes down and when you inhale the code goes up. Each inhale and exhale count as one time.

Relax and breathe.

It is done.

<u>NOTE</u>

You may eventually see the image pulsating, moving or change color on the screen or feel tingling sensations in the body. These are all part of the activation.

After the visualization, meditate for 11 minutes and take notes of your perceptions and any awakening revelations.

For the next 7 days, drink abundant pure water to support the body to integrate the transformation and journal your experiences.

EPILOGUE

Everyone has his own specific vocation or mission in life; everyone must carry out a concrete assignment that demands fulfillment. Therein he cannot be replaced, nor can his life be repeated, thus, everyone's task is unique as his specific opportunity to implement it. ~Victor Frankl

As our assignment from the masters is completed, Now, we pass the torch, the fire of this mission to you, as it is *Your Turn* to become an emissary of these transmissions and to share whatever served you from these messages here received.
The purpose to expand our minds and hearts is to receive and share with all sentient beings the energy of Omni love and to become a model of the pure embodiment of eternal presence.

May these messages , its transmission and the ways these will serve your life, expand our minds and hearts and merge these in to the eternal ocean of consciousness that is ever present.

From being and becoming and back to being.
I salute your strength, the timeliness and timelessness of your existence. You are the greatest teacher, the greatest emissary of light, the living code, and the active transmission of God's living message.

May you walk your path unplugged from the illusory
and Be the gift that you came here to be
for without You existence would not be complete.

Here is a test to find whether your mission on Earth is finished:
If you're alive, it isn't.
~ Richard Bach

Namaste

Ivonne Delaflor Alexander

ASCENDED MASTERS REFERENCES

During the weeks that followed the first message, more and more names of Masters showed up that we were not able to identify, beyond what was given to Ivonne upon receiving the messages. We decided not to offer any interpretations or guess at the identity, as we realized that the message is more important than the messenger.

Abraham
Abraham is the eponym of the Abrahamic religions, among which are Judaism, Christianity and Islam. According to both the Hebrew Bible and the Qur'an, through his sons Ishmael and Isaac, Abraham is the forefather of many tribes, namely the Ishmaelites, Israelites, Midianites and Edomites. Abraham was a descendant of Noah's son, Shem. Christians believe that Jesus was a descendant of Abraham through Isaac, and Muslims believe that Muhammad was a descendant of Abraham through Ishmael. Abraham is notable for his advocation and promotion of monotheism. www.crystalinks.com

Ah Mon Rha
This ascended master spoke to Ivonne Delaflor through the process of automatic writing for the book *Unplug Your Mind*.

Ah-Mhan-Tat
Great Father Founder Council of AH.

Ahu, Rah Gestalt
This ascended master spoke to Ivonne Delaflor through the process of automatic writing for the book *Unplug Your Mind*.

Archangel Gabriel
Is known as the messenger of God, helps with messenger work, naturally. Gabriel assists writers, teachers, and communicators, especially journalists. If you want to complete a book project, call on Gabriel. This angel is what I affectionately call a "nudging angel," and she will push you along to get your book done. By Doreen Virtue.

Archangel Metatron
Or Master Metatron, one of major Archangels, as well as Chief Elohim. Assigned by Mother/Father God to be in charge of this present Creation, which is sixth of ten Creations provided for by Divine Plan. He is the twin brother of the angel Sandalphon. He was Enoch in an earthly incarnation. Metatron Messages from the "Keys of Enoch", Metatron is called the Almighty Eternal Lord and Divine Voice of the Father. Considered the Creator of the outer worlds, a teacher and guide to Enoch and creator of the Keys. He is also a co-worker with Zoroaster. Greatdreams.com/masters

Archangel Michael
Earth's representative of the all-encompassing strength of the Divine. Michael lends you support, courage, and confidence. He'll boost your resolve to make healthy changes, as well as guide you to new opportunities and help you heal from past experiences. From "The Miracles of Archangel Michael" by Doreen Virtue.

Archangel Rafael
Is always available to help renew your health. Whether you're fighting a cold or trying to forgive a friend's hurtful comments, turn to Raphael for guidance on restoring your body and mind. By Doreen Virtue.

Babaji Nagaraj
Ascended Master Representative Guest at the Council of AH.
Babaji is recognized in the spiritual world as the ageless Sidda (adept), omniscient, omnipotent and omnipresent who was introduced to Westerners in the book, Autobiography of a Yogi, written by Pramahansa Yogananda. The meaning in English for Babaji is "Venerable Father." It is said by those who have met Babaji, that he is the Param Sidda (Supreme Perfected Being) who has achieved a state free from death limitations. He can travel through time and space as he wishes with or without a physical body. Babaji is immortal. It is said that he never lives in the same place for more than seven days. He travels from place to place in the northern Himalayan Mountains with his select group of disciples. He easily can speak in any language. His immortal body does not require food; therefore he seldom eats. His mission is love. And it is said that

when his name is pronounced with love, humbleness and reverence an immediate blessing is received. Om Babaji Namaha. www.maitriorder.com

Brother Issa (Jesus)
It was told to humanity that Jesus or Jesus Christ was born in 2-6 BCE in Bethlehem, Judea. Little is known about his early life, but as a young man, he founded Christianity, one of the world's most influential religions. His life is recorded in the New Testament, more a theological document than a biography. According to Christians, Jesus is considered the incarnation of God and his teachings an example for living a more spiritual life. Christians believe he died for the sins of all people and rose from the dead. www.biography.com

Brother Paul
This ascended master spoke to Ivonne Delaflor through the process of automatic writing for the book *Unplug Your Mind*. There is no assumption or claim that the named being, Paul, is or is not Saint Paul, an apostle of Jesus or Paul the Venetian, another ascended master.

Buddha
Lord Gautama - the Buddha, was one of the great enlightened ones. He taught detachment and the middle way. The Buddha represents the wisdom energy while Christ is the love energy and they are brother\sister equal energies. Ascended 2500 years ago, Buddha "gave it all up" to find meaning in life and the reason why some suffered so much. It was during a meditation under the Bodhi Tree that he received Enlightenment. Buddhism was formed out of his Teachings. www.greatdreams.com

Community at the Service of the Great Father of Sirius
This ascended master spoke to Ivonne Delaflor through the process of automatic writing for the book *Unplug Your Mind*.

Council of AH
Decision-making body in AH, the Higher Universe of Earth, which is located beyond the 15 dimensional Time Matrix. Also called the Absolute harmonic Universe.

Cuathli Aguila Exche
This ascended master spoke to Ivonne Delaflor through the process of automatic writing for the book *Unplug Your Mind*.

Djwal Khul
Or Brother Djwal, was a Tibetan and known by the name Gai Ben-Jamin in his youth in the early part of The Theosophical Society, that was before he became an Adept. He is often referred to as the Master D. K. and is also known as "The Tibetan". www.ascension-research.org

Eah-Rtha
Gestalt Founder Mothers & Fathers of Earth.

Eh-Nah-Yah-El
Quantum Scholar Council of AH.

Equileh Ah Rah Meh
Honorary Guardian Observant of The Laws of AH

Ezekiel
Was a priest living with the Jewish exiles in Babylon after the taking of Judah and Jerusalem by Babylon, around 580-600 B.C. Like other prophets, Ezekiel says that God is very dismayed by worship of idols and "gods" and at "false prophets" and hypocrites (for example, Eziekiel 7:3; 14:10). Like Jeremiah, Ezekiel believed that the old doctrine of children being punished for their father's sins was wrong. So, Ezekiel was saying that "...a righteous man who does what is just and right...he will surely live." (Ezekiel 18:5-9). www.biblenotes.net

Father Hu-Nab, Kum
This ascended master spoke to Ivonne Delaflor through the process of automatic writing for the book *Unplug Your Mind*.

G-Hay-El-Hi
Physics Tao Guardian, Council of AH.

Gah-Ehl-Rah
Master Emissary of Mind-physics of AH.

Grand Father Jaguar
This ascended master spoke to Ivonne Delaflor through the process of automatic writing for the book *Unplug Your Mind*.

Ha-Ehl-Yeh
AH Guardian of Universal Emissaries of Light Council of AH.

Hay Merth Hau Hu
Honorary Guardian of the Law of Cause and Effect, Member of the Council of AH.

Hel-Tha-Hu
Universal Architect Engineer, Member of the Council of AH.

Hermes
Hermes was known in ancient times as the great sage to whom is attributed sacred writings and alchemical and astrological works. Because of his learning and profound skill in the art and sciences, the Egyptians gave him the name Trismegistus, which means "thrice-great" and also applies to his role as philosopher, priest and king. This ascended master is also known as the God Mercury. Hermes walked the earth for tens of thousands of years. Hermes Trismegistus has been referred to as the father of alchemy. According to one legend, a slab of emerald found in his tomb had inscribed upon it Hermes' precepts for making gold. This emerald tablet contained the familiar Hermetic axiom: "What is below is like that which is above. And what is above is like that which is below." From "The Masters and their Retreats," by Mark L. Prophet and Elizabeth Clare Prophet.

Hilarion
The Ascended Master Hilarion is the Chohan of the Fifth Ray. He embodies the qualities of healing and wholeness, music and science, and one-pointed vision (the action of the third-eye). His retreat is in the etheric octave above Crete, Greece. At his retreat, Hilarion prepares

us to receive the gift of healing. The apostle Paul was one of Hilarion's incarnations. www.greatdreams.com/masters

Hunab Kah Hul
Quantum Chief Soul Creator Medical Universal Scientist Guest Honor for the Council of AH.

Isaiah
Or Brother Isaiah, was a Biblical prophet who lived in the land of Judah c. 740 - 681 BC. Prophets such as Isaiah were said to have a special message from God. The message Isaiah was delivering mainly concerned the rebellious nature of God's chosen people Israel, as recorded in the Old Testament book of Isaiah. www.thenagain.info

Isis
Isis, the Egyptian goddess of rebirth remains one of the most familiar images of empowered and utter femininity. The goddess Isis was the first daughter of Geb, god of the Earth, and Nut, the goddess of the Overarching Sky. Isis was born on the first day between the first years of creation, and was adored by her human followers. The ancient Egyptian goddess Isis has many gifts to share with modern women. Isis embodies the strengths of the feminine, the capacity to feel deeply about relationships, the act of creation, and the source of sustenance and protection. www.goddessgift.com

J.K
This ascended master spoke to Ivonne Delaflor through the process of automatic writing for the book *Unplug Your Mind*.

Kah-Mah-Ehl
Wisdom Elder Council of AH.

Lord Kuthumi
The Master Kuthumi sometimes spelled Koot Hoomi, Kut Humi, rarely Kut-Hu-Mi, Master K.H., or simply K.H. in Theosophy, is regarded as one of the "Masters of the Ancient Wisdom." According to Theosophy, Kuthumi is considered to be one of the members of the

Spiritual Hierarchy called the Masters of the Ancient Wisdom, which oversees the development of the human race on this planet to higher levels of consciousness. In the Ascended Master Teachings, Kuthumi is one of the Ascended Masters who collectively make up the Great White Brotherhood. Kuthumi is also known as a Mahatma and is regarded as the Master of the Second Ray. www.crystalinks.com

Kwan Yin
Known as The Goddess of Mercy, Gentle Protector, Bodhisattva of Compassion, even the savior of seamen and fishermen, she holds many titles. The spelling of her name varies, but it is not so much the arrangement of letters as it is the effect that her spoken name produces on those with a Buddhist background, similar to a reaction in the West when one is speaking of the Virgin Mary. In both cases, it invokes the feeling of compassion and unconditional love. www.mykwanyin.com

Lady Nada
Ascended Lady Master Nada is Chohan of the Sixth Ray, the purple and gold ray, of peace, service and brotherhood. She tutors souls in mastering these qualities in the solar-plexus chakra, and helps them prepare to receive the Holy Spirit's gifts of speaking in tongues and interpretation of tongues. In addition, she is known as the unifier of families and twin flames. The word Nada means the voice of the silence. Nada is a Messenger of the Lord Meru and received training in his retreat. Nada has a certain cosmic authority for the incoming age. Healing is one of Her actions or services to mankind. She is one who directs healing to the mankind of Earth. She uses a Pink Flame for some of Her work. Nada is a member of the Karmic Board and represents the Third Ray in that body. She has recently assumed the Chohanship for the Sixth Ray for the time being. Her symbol is a pink rose. www.greatdreams.com/masters

Lha-Tzah-EH
Honorary member Council of AH.

Lord Matreya
Matreya or Maitreya. The Name "Maitreya" means "Lord of Love". Maitreya embodied upon Earth millions of years ago as a volunteer

(guardian) from the planet Venus responding to beloved Sanat Kumara's pledge to raise our planet's humanity up out of the degenerate state to which it had descended. Maitreya reached His greatest attainment in the Light of God while embodied with Lord Himalaya. He enfolded Jesus in His Cosmic Flame to assist Jesus in manifesting the Christ Consciousness. (ascension-research.org)

M.Krishna
Krishna is Sanskrit for "the all-attractive Person." It is a name frequently used to refer to the Supreme Being in some of the Vedic writings of India, especially those dealing with the science of devotion to God like the Srimad-Bhagavatam and the Bhagavad Gita. They explain that Krishna is the original supreme person, the Absolute Truth, the ultimate source of all energies and of all other incarnations of God. www.krishna.com

MA
This ascended master spoke to Ivonne Delaflor through the process of automatic writing for the book *Unplug Your Mind*.

Mary
This ascended master spoke to Ivonne Delaflor through the process of automatic writing for the book *Unplug Your Mind*.
There is no assumption or claim that the named being Mary, is or is not Mother Mary or Mary Magdalene.

Mary Magdalene.
Mary Magdalene represented the Great-Goddess-Mother-Queen, wife of "Jesus." Historically, it is said she was the daughter of Juba II, the black-skinned King of Mauretania and wife, Queen Cleopatra Selene (daughter of Antony and Cleopatra). It was told to humanity that Mary Magdalene was one of the most devoted of Jesus' followers, always by his side and *'ministered to him of her substance.'* She attended him to Calvary, stood weeping at the foot of the cross, and was the first to see the Christ risen. Extra-biblical and Gnostic traditions about Mary Magdalene holds that she was the wife of Jesus and pregnant with his child at the time of his death, a fact which was omitted by later revisionist editors of the Gospels. Interpreted allegorically, Luke-Acts reveals their marriage, a

daughter, and two sons. http://www.thenazareneway.com/life_of_st_mary_magdalene.htm

Master Ebeelon
This ascended master spoke to Ivonne Delaflor through the process of automatic writing for the book *Unplug Your Mind*.

Master Kybalion
This ascended master spoke to Ivonne Delaflor through the process of automatic writing for the book *Unplug Your Mind*. There is no assumption or claim regarding the story or history of this being, other than the known reference of the book which carries the same name: Kybalion. The Kybalion is a written work based upon the very old Hermetic Teachings founded by Hermes Trismegistus, known by the Ancient Egyptians as "The Great, Great" and "Master of Masters".

Mataji
Guest Honorary Earth Mechanics Consultant for the Council of AH
Mataji means "Holy Mother". It is said that Mataji is the immortal sister of Babaji. Sri Mataji has also lived through the centuries; she is almost as far advanced spiritually as her brother. She remains in ecstasy in a hidden underground cave near the Dasasamedh ghat. From *Autobiography of a Yogi* by Paramhansa Yogananda.

Rah-Mah-El
This ascended master spoke to Ivonne Delaflor through the process of automatic writing for the book *Unplug Your Mind*.

Saint Germaine
Chohan of the Seventh Ray (there are seven rays of the White Light that emerge through the prism of the Christ Consciousness), the violet ray, of freedom, alchemy, justice, mercy and transmutation. He is the sponsor of the United States of America and the hierarch of the Age of Aquarius, who comes bearing the gift of the violet flame for world change. He tutors and initiates souls in mastery of the seat-of-the-soul chakra, preparing them to receive the Holy Spirit's gifts of prophecy and the working of miracles. Two of his well-known embodiments were

Christopher Columbus and Merlin the magician, a spiritual adept who has unfortunately been mythologized. Saint Germaine teaches that the highest alchemy is the transformation of one's human consciousness into the divinity of the Higher Self. Greatdreams.com/masters.

Sanat Kumara
According to Church Universal and Triumphant, the Sanat Kumara is the leader of mankind. According to certain esoteric, mystic and gnostic traditions, Sanat Kumara (eternal youth in Sanskrit) and 144,000 souls from planet Venus came to Earth in her darkest hour to hold the light of God. Notable beings in the 144,000 include Jesus, Gautama Buddha, and Maitreya Buddha. www.crystalinks.com

Sath, Kam
AH First Officer of the Council of AH.

Serapis Bay
An ascended master associated with Luxor in Egypt, who holds open the Temple doors on the etheric level, and is one of the great teachers of ascension on the planet. Serapis Bey originally came from Venus and is the Keeper of the White Flame. He works with Archangel Chamuel on the Ray of Compassion and is the only Ascended Master who works with the Seraphim. He has an ascension seat Luxor. www.greatdreams.com

Siddharta
See "Buddha"

Tah-Tah-Yeh
Great Grandfather Founder of Gaia.

The Father Tah-Tah
Great Founder Father of AH.

The Mother OMAH
Great One Mother of AH.

The Nameless
The Nameless One. It is said that he is a being from out the Great Central Sun.
The Masters and their Retreats, by Mark Prophet and Elisabeth Clare Prophet.

White Brotherhood Gestalt
A spiritual organization of the Ascended Masters; a highly evolved united consciousness assisting Earth and Humanity to ascend.

Yeshua Ha Yuh
Guardian Omni Love Field Frequencies Counselor for the Council of AH.

ABOUT THE AUTHORS

Ivonne Delaflor, also known as Swami Amenai is the founder and president of Delaflor Teachings International, founder of Mastery Life A.C. and co-founder of the Higher School for Conscious Evolution. She is the author of *The Positive Child through the Language of Love, Mastering Life, Sacred Messages for the Parents of the World, Divine Mother, India: The Journey of a Lifetime, Invitation to Love* and others. Ivonne has published several articles for Tibetan women's magazines, Integral Life and several E-zine articles on leadership, synergy and the importance of self-actualization.

She is a certified Total Awareness Coach and certified Parent Talk trainer and has studied Sacred Shamanic Rebirth, Body Language, Constellation Therapy, Breath Therapy, and is a Reiki Master. She has done more than 500 hours of personal work at BEBA, a non-profit organization that supports healthy bonding and attachment for infants and their parents and is a graduate of The School for The Work with Byron Katie, and the Futuring School with Stefan Hermann. She is also a graduate of the Platinum Mentoring Coaching with Brian Tracy, has a career in Fitness and Nutrition ,is a certified RAW Nutritionist from the School of David Wolfe, and has a Master's Degree in Business Administration.

Ivonne is the creator of The Codes of AH ©, Sacred Geometrical Mandalas that have been said to support the healing of many ailments and enhance meditation and self healing skills for all who use them.

Ivonne has been initiated into Babaji's ancient Kriya Yoga tradition and received initiations (shaktipat) directly from Babaji, whom she met one-on-one in Rishikesh, India, in the year 2003. She was also initiated as Swami Amenanda, lovingly called by students and friends Amenai, receiving her name by direct request of Babaji Nagaraj. She is an initiate of the Maitri Violet-Silver Chord Order

In 2006, she created the Transcendental Rebirthing System, supporting ecstatic rebirth of the whole being into brilliancy and re-patterning awareness, healing old traumas and reorganizing ancestral legacies.

She offers free webinars, live workshops and the ten-day Intensive Certification Program of Transcendental Rebirthing offered once a year. She offers private sessions and through her Diamond Mentorship Program supports many women to set their mission in motion and live a life of brilliance. She also creates personalized sacred Codes of AH© and offers a monthly live free gathering of teachings in her own home.

She is a supporter of raising awareness about, Healthy Food Choices, Earth Reconnection, Autism and Eating Disorders and educates people on these very important issues in humanity.

Ivonne's mission is to empower, teach, motivate, guide and share ancient wisdom translated into easy modern ways that anyone can use for their own self-realization and betterment of their lives, their families, their communities and contribution to the world; herein Ivonne finds her passion for living.

Ivonne currently shares her time with her three children and her beloved husband and life partner, Toby Alexander.

Sylvia Dokter is a professional personal transformation coach, teacher and intuitive healer. She is the founder of Rebirthing In Joy, co-founder of Epic Goddess and Sacred Baby Steps, VP of Delaflor Teachings International and founder of Executive Awareness Productions.

Born in Amsterdam, the Netherlands, and with a background in Sociology, Sylvia started her professional life in the international trade environment of Paris, France. In 1996 she decided to branch out from the business world and to start her own journey of personal discovery. Her curiosity and adventurous nature led her to a wide range of studies and trainings.

The end of 2007 was a turning point for Sylvia. The inspiring and transcendental teachings in the field of the quantum physics from the founders of the Higher School for Conscious Evolution, Ivonne and Toby Alexander, provided the necessary tools to complete her search for the most powerful (self)healing and self realization studies. Over the next 5 years she became certified as a Transcendental Rebirthing Master Trainer Level 4, Codeologist, DNA Master Activation Practitioner, and Diamond Mentorship Program(DMP) coach.

Besides mental and spiritual studies she also developed a fascination for the central nervous system in relation to restore inner balance through energetic bodywork by combining her qualities as a Cranio Sacral Facilitator, Reiki Master, Spinal Column Release Facilitator and Foot Reflexologist. She is a Bach Flower Remedies Practitioner and Trainer, Health Practitioner, Doula (birth attendant), Numerological Profiler (as per the JJ.Erdosi system), Color and Geomantic analyzer, Interior Designer and a Feng Shui Consultant. She has also studied NLP & Career Counseling, and family constellation dynamics. Her love for and skill to communicate (telepathically) with animals led her to become an Animal (behavior) therapist.

She is initiated as Swami Bhimananda into the Silver Violet Maitri-Order and received an initiation into Sri Babaji's ancient Kriya Yoga.

Sylvia is committed to support humanity on their journey in raising their frequencies toward the state of joy, by combining knowledge, love, healing and service. She lives currently in Cancun, Mexico and offers sessions and trainings all over the world to support others to increase self awareness and recognize one's own greatness.

OTHER BOOKS BY THE AUTHORS

Author Ivonne Delaflor Alexander

You can find the books of Ivonne Delaflor Alexander at all online book retailers or by emailing us at hsfce@higherschoolforconsciousevolution.com.

The Book of Origins – Paperback (Mar. 11, 2011) by Ivonne Delaflor. What if there was a place in the universe, or in another universe, where no evil forces, dark beliefs, negative thought projections, energy blockages, or control issues were present? Is there a place such as an intact field of light, benevolence, and love? In *The Book of Origins*, author Ivonne Delaflor presents lessons she received that propose a new vision of a universe, in which harmony is seen not as something to fight for, but as a natural ebb and flow of events through the choices we make. Throughout a period of five years, Delaflor received more than five thousand messages during conversations with her transpersonal masters. In this text, she does not interpret the lessons but rather shares selected messages in order to help people form better relationships with their inner voices and make sense of their spiritual experiences. A clear and readable map for navigating the harmonic energy dimensions, *The Book of Origins* supports humanity within the inner ascension process as we evolve as species of consciousness in the here and now and beyond.

India: The Journey of a Lifetime - Paperback (Mar. 7, 2005) by Ivonne Delaflor. "How do you describe a cool spring rain on your face? Impossible! That's how it is when I try to describe what it feels like to be in India. Most words seem useless; adjectives that might otherwise be appropriate miss the mark. I have felt this way for a long time until I read Ivonne Delaflor's book *India, The Journey of a Lifetime*. Finally, someone else was able to describe the magic, beauty, mystery and heart of India that so many others have failed to fully capture. This book is an opportunity to see the guru in every face. This is the message her books impart more than any other: God, lessons and love are everywhere…in each smile, frown, smell, noise and moment. It's what India teaches us. It's what Ivonne

surely understands and amazingly communicates to us about a mystical journey through this unique and mysterious continent."
-Maggie Rauen, Co-Founder of the Peace by Piece Project, Santa Barbara, CA.

Your Soulmate Called God - Paperback (Mar. 16, 2005) by Ivonne Delaflor.
You cannot help but to be impacted by this remarkable woman, a powerful model of love in action. Now she has produced the book you hold in your hands that puts into words her deeply felt personal experience and relationship with God. She describes how the first part was written following a conversation with a friend, which inspired her to write for hours in a beautiful reverie of poetic expression. The second was scribed during an emotional valley, a period of sorrow and depression. Each of these experiences demonstrated that the source of enduring love and joy is not to be found in another person or in materiality, but instead through discovering your true soulmate—God.
Be sure to savor these writings, sipping a little here and there like a fine wine. Breathe slowly as you read each piece. Let the words permeate your consciousness and open your physical senses to the ecstatic experience of the Divine. Doing so will allow you to remember the eternal being that you are, and your heart will sing as you find union with your one and only true Soulmate called God.
- Dr. Steven Farmer Ph.D, author of Sacred Ceremony and Power Animals. Excerpt from the foreword to *Your Soulmate Called God*.

Invitation To Love: 108 Reminders for the Enlightened Ones - Paperback (Jan. 26, 2005) by Ivonne Delaflor.
Follow the Sanatan Dharma, the Eternal Religion of Prema, Divine Love, and the one and only that can only be found in your heart. And remember: YOU must guide others to it through love, simplicity and truth. That is the only way. That is the unspoken, eternal and nameless way. Always remember that no time is ever wasted except for the time that one is not loving. Move out of the house of ignorance! There are better places to live. Ring, ring! Wake up! The Buddha nature and Christ-like energy within are ready to be reawakened in all. Become like a child! Enter the kingdom of heaven. The Christ and Buddha nature are within! So, where is the kingdom?

Excerpted from *Invitation to Love*.
"The greatest blessing in my life was the gift of being in the physical presence of Babaji in Herrekhan in 1980. One day he said that he would be leaving his body, I asked him if he would still come to me if I asked. He simply looked at me and smiled knowingly and said: "Of course!" Recently, my work healing moved to a new level. Some of the recent miracles have been so powerful as to leave me shaky. I could only turn to God to keep myself stable and humble; and so I asked for his advice. Well, he has answered my request. And I imagine he will answer the prayers of many others, through the writings of Ivonne Delaflor. In them I recognize his voice, his humor, his teaching. Thank you Babaji! And thank you Ivonne for being such an open channel!"
Dan Brulé

The Positive Child: Through the Language of Love - Paperback (Sept. 23, 2004) by Ivonne Delaflor. In 1988, Ivonne Delaflor had an accident that changed her perception of life forever. After a near death experience, she began to listen to her higher guides and the voice of God and began to pursue, with grand courage, her spiritual journey. Ivonne Delaflor is a certified trainer of The Parent Talk System created by Mr. Chick Moorman, and teaches meditation classes to young children in Cancun, Mexico. She is the mother of two children.
Ivonne is the Creator of the Mastery Life non-profit organization that is constantly researching the evolution and the sharing of spiritual life. As a passionate child advocate, her mission is to assist all children throughout the world to never ever forget who they are. She offers regular seminars, conferences and workshops for parents in Cancun, Mexico and assists others to do so.

Mastering Life: Co-creating a Reality of Love Through the Power of Sharing - Paperback (Jan. 5, 2005) by Ivonne Delaflor.
From the Foreword by Alan Cohen: "The lessons here in Mastering Life keep pointing us back to the simplicity of loving. We find ourselves in a world where complexity seems to pull us from joy at every turn. Simply holding the consciousness of love will open doors that anxious striving cannot. Behold the answer that sooths, heals, uplifts and changes the world, beginning with ourselves.

"Take your time as you stroll through these insightful pages. Absorb the words and images and make them your own. While they seem to be teaching you, they are really reminding you of what you know deep inside your heart. Then bring the principles to life in your own unique way and enjoy the blessings they deliver."

Divine Mother: Devotional Offerings for the Sacred Feminine within All Beings - Paperback (July 19, 2007) by Ivonne Delaflor.
"Without the Divine Mother principle incorporated into one's concept of 'God,' half the story regarding divine nature is not told."
—Toby Alexander, author of *The Great Master*
Ivonne Delaflor's stunning collection of devotional poems sets in motion the Divine Feminine within your consciousness so that her compassion and wisdom will become a part of you. The poetry, the stories, the prayers, and the higher invocations included in this collection are not only about God as the feminine force in heaven, but are also *for* the God in everyone and everything—the feminine in each flower, each living creature, and each cell. The Divine Feminine lives in all creation. Whether you are male or female, let *Divine Mother* reawaken the Divine Feminine energies within you.

Sacred Messages for the Parents of the World - Paperback (Feb. 19, 2006) by Ivonne Delaflor and Phil LaHaye.
Parents TRUST that if you are reading this book right now…[it] is mainly because your inner child and your children are vibrating in a higher frequency of love and growing in awareness to create a most conscious world.
Your studies, your PhD's and mental knowledge are useless now. It is time to bring forth the wisdom of the ancients. It is time to show the spiritual face of the human existence. Many in the multiple universes are ready. Are you ready?
Time to shake the illusory world! The children have arrived. -Excerpted from *Sacred Messages for the Parents of the World*.
As with all sacred texts, they have been given to the human race to guide us to be the God-like beings that we are here to learn how to be. This book is now given to us as a sacred text to help us guide our children from the moment they are conceived, as well as ourselves, into God-

Consciousness. "The real war in this era is not in the battlefield, but in families." This book will help you to open the many gates of love in your families, in your world, and in your heart.

Stop Wasting Your Time and Start Doing What Matters Most: A Wake-Up Call for True Leadership [Paperback], Jeffrey Krug (Author), Ivonne Delaflor Alexander (Author)

People who believe that they have no time and who lack the awareness of values, time management and goal setting, tend to be followers. They procrastinate, they usually don't care to contribute to the higher good, and they live in a comfort zone with no vision or plan for a better future. They live their lives in a blurry world where opportunities are missed and the promise of success is blocked. In *Stop Wasting Your Time & Start Doing What Matters Most! A Wake-Up Call for True Leadership*, you will gain new awareness and learn how to use success strategies and the art of goal setting in deciding how you spend your time and thereby transcend the limits of possibilities for your future. True and good leaders understand and rely on these tools to achieve success. Are you a true leader? Are you prepared to make a significant difference in your life and the lives of those around you? If you are ready to find the answers within yourself; if you are willing to start doing what matters most; and if you want to leave a legacy of power, synergy, and higher values to the children of humanity, then this is the book for you. This is your wake-up call for true leadership. "The way you determine your values and organize your priorities determines everything you achieve as a leader- and this book gives you a wonderful blueprint to do just that" -Brian Tracy, author of How the Best Leaders Lead.

SUGGESTED READING; TO FURTHER YOUR CONNECTION WITH HIGHER WORLDS

Alexander, Toby. *The Great Master.* Iuniverse, 2008. (Higher inquiry, decrees, and holistic inspirations in preparation for the awakening of the Masters of the Great Work here on Planet Earth.)

Allen, James. *As a Man Thinketh.* Tremendous Life Books, 2001.

Balangoda Ananda Maitreya(Translator), Thich Nhat Hanh(Foreword). *The Dhammapada.* Parallax Press, August 1, 1995. (423 verses of the Buddha.)

Lao-tzu. *The Tao Te Ching.* Vintage, 1989.

Paramhansa Yogananda. *Autobiography of a Yogi.* The Philosophical Library Inc., 1946.

Talbot, Michael. *The Holographic Universe.* Harper Perennial; Reprint edition September 6, 2011

Three Initiates. *The Kybalion. 1912-1914.* (A study of the Hermetic Philosophy of ancient Egypt and Greece.)

SUGGESTED LINKS

www.Ivonnedelaflor.com

www.rebirthinginjoy.com

www.higherschoolforconsciousevolution.com

www.dnaperfection.com

www.transcendentalrebirthing.com

www.sacredbabysteps.com

www.beyourbrilliancenow.com

Find us on Facebook:
https://www.facebook.com/HSFCE
https://www.facebook.com/UnplugYourMind

Follow us on Twitter:
https: twitter.com/Amenai

Subscribe to our free blog:
http://rawnestliving.wordpress.com/

NOTES

Printed in Great Britain
by Amazon